GOD IN ACTION

GOD IN ACTION

Theological Addresses

BY KARL BARTH

PROFESSOR IN THE UNIVERSITY OF BASEL
BASEL, SWITZERLAND

English Translation by

E. G. HOMRIGHAUSEN

MINISTER, EVANGELICAL AND REFORMED CHURCH
LECTURER, BUTLER UNIVERSITY, INDIANAPOLIS

KARL J. ERNST

PROFESSOR OF EXEGESIS
MISSION HOUSE THEOLOGICAL SEMINARY, PLYMOUTH

Introduction by

JOSIAS FRIEDLI

PROFESSOR OF CHURCH HISTORY
MISSION HOUSE THEOLOGICAL SEMINARY, PLYMOUTH

TRANSLATION AUTHORIZED AND APPROVED BY KARL BARTH
AND CHRISTIAN KAISER VERLAG, MUNICH

Wipf & Stock
PUBLISHERS
Eugene, Oregon

Wipf and Stock Publishers
199 W 8th Ave, Suite 3
Eugene, OR 97401

God In Action
By Barth, Karl
Copyright©1936 Theologischer Verlag Zurich
ISBN: 1-59752-426-3
Publication date 11/1/2005
Previously published by Round Table Press, Inc, 1936

Copyright©1936 Original German version published by
Theologischer Verlag Zurich

FOREWORD

THESE chapters are a collection of addresses delivered by Karl Barth to various groups. Since the discontinuance of the periodical *Zwischen den Zeiten,* he and Eduard Thurneysen have edited a series of pamphlets entitled *Theologische Existenz Heute.* These addresses were published in the latter series of pamphlets in different numbers.

The three addresses, on "Revelation," "Church," and "Theology," Professor Barth explains, "were delivered by invitation of the Free Protestant Theological Faculty in Paris, France, from April tenth to twelfth, 1934."

The address on "The Ministry of the Word of God" was "delivered on September eleventh, 1934, at a meeting of pastors of the western section of Switzerland in Vaumarcus, Canton Neufchatel, in French, and redelivered in the original German on September twelfth at Pratteln, Canton Baselland, at a pastors' conference." The theme of the address was assigned to Professor Barth by those who sponsored the meeting in western Switzerland. It touches upon something quite akin to the subject of the last chapter in this book concerning the Christian as a witness, which was published as number twelve in the *Theologische Existenz Heute*.

The chapter on "The Christian as Witness" is a "stenographic report of an address delivered on the seventh of August, 1934, at the International Summer Conference for Students at La Chataigneraie, near Coppett, in Canton Vaud, Switzerland." This theme was also assigned to Professor Barth.

The "Appendix" contains "added stenographic reports of the discussions which followed the address on 'The Christian as Witness.' The German language was used both in the addresses and the discussions. But two interpreters, well versed in the subject matter and in their respective languages, rendered them into French and English."

E. G. H.

TABLE OF CONTENTS

INTRODUCTION

AMERICAN religious leaders are beginning to manifest a new interest in basic theological problems. The reasons for this are quite evident. Our feverish activism, our easy optimism, and our confidence in automatic inevitable progress have been severely shaken and have given place to a feeling of helpless bewilderment. It is in such times of confusion and uncertainty that men seek the deeper realities of life. The periods of great theological vigor were also the periods of widespread confusion and disorder. Augustine wrote his *Confessions* while the Roman empire was breaking under the pressure of the invading barbarians. Calvin's *Institutes* came out of the religious and political turmoil of his time and was written in flight from political injustice. The great vital productive ages in the history of the Church were the "creed-making," not the "creed-reciting" ages. It is when men wrestle with truth, when they face the deepest problems of life, which are always theological, that the Church is established through the witness to the truth.

Of course, we still have those who have "done" with theology—though as a matter of fact they never began. But there is a growing number among us, who are earnestly seeking sounder foundations, who are looking away from the frail supports of man-made plans and human ways, unto the living God revealed in Jesus Christ. To such these chapters will be a welcome aid in their search.

These chapters will also be of interest to those who are trying to learn what Karl Barth stands for in the theological world. For the English reader it has been difficult to obtain first-hand information, especially as to Barth's positive and constructive theology. Much, indeed, has been written about him, but both his friends and his foes, by their interpretations and criticisms, have frequently beclouded the real issues. The two volumes of sermons by Barth and Thurneysen have done much to acquaint the English reader with the religious ideas of the movement. They have demonstrated that this theology can be translated into soul-searching, pungent sermons, which is ever the final test of any theological system.

This volume is not presented as a complete system of Barthian theology. Nevertheless, the table of contents will show that the subjects have been selected with a view to presenting the main theological contributions which Barth has made to our generation. The selection was made from a series of brochures, published under the title of *Theologische Existenz Heute,* edited by Karl Barth and Eduard Thurneysen. These brochures are mostly lectures delivered before eager groups of ministers, and addresses and sermons before large audiences. They are, therefore, not merely the academic product of the professor's sanctum but issue from the battlefront of an intense religious struggle, at a time when it is not "all quiet on the western front." The chapter on the Church reveals with refreshing clarity Barth's position in the German church conflict. He simply holds to a definite conception of the Church. He does not antagonize any form or theory of government. He is not crusading against socialism or communism. He is not concerned with theories of government or policies of administration but with God and

His Church. His Church stands there like a rock in a surging sea. It may be a storm center; the roar of many waters may resound mightily; the foamy billows may rise high, and even for a time submerge it; all this not because the rock has gone out to battle the sea but because the sea has struck something solid.

Those who grasp Barth's ideas regarding Revelation, the Church, the Christian Ministry, etc., will see why one cannot properly speak of "Barthianism" or a "Barthian School." The whole emphasis is on something beyond Barth or any group of men. Barth is a *witness* to the truth and a witness is of only relative significance.

But it is not the purpose of the introduction to interpret Barth or the contents of this book. The important thing is that Barth here speaks for himself. There is good reason to believe that the English-speaking public will be glad for the opportunity to hear him. The translators, as well as the author, have no other aim than to bear witness to the truth, for the glory of God.

JOSIAS FRIEDLI.

Mission House, 1935.

GOD IN ACTION

REVELATION

WE CANNOT speak of revelation without being made immediately aware of two other concepts which are closely related to it. They are the concepts of testimony and confession. We would not know of revelation if it did not come to us by way of testimony concerning it. I mean by this the word and the spirit of the apostles and prophets as they live in the Holy Scriptures. The Church is founded on revelation through the medium of the testimony of those who have heard and seen it. In faith we can have knowledge of it, and speak of it for the very reason that this testimony exists. To receive and accept revelation means, then, to receive and accept this testimony. And this in turn constitutes confession. We cannot speak of revelation as we speak of the results of philosophic reflections on ourselves and on the presuppositions of our existence, or as we speak of discoveries in the spheres of nature

[3]

and history. We cannot maintain its reality and truth as if *we* had discovered it, and as if we could establish its validity. We can only receive, accept, and acknowledge it on the ground of the testimony concerning it which has created the Church, and still preserves it, and in which it, namely, revelation, meets us in its own power, credibility, and authority.

Let me elucidate in a parable the relation of the three concepts of revelation, testimony, and confession; and chiefly the reality and truth of what we are to understand by revelation.

On the battlefield (namely, not in a study, nor on a stage but on the battlefield of human life) *it has happened* (it has indubitably and irrevocably happened with the complete, once-for-all singularity [Einmaligkeit] and with the whole gravity of a factual event) *that the enemy* (the enemy, the other one, not man himself but his opponent, an adversary who is determined to engage man) *with overwhelming superiority* (the event is caused by *his* intention and disposition and not by man's) *has gone into action* (we are not asked if and how we intend to come to grips with him, for the engagement is in full swing). This event is God's revelation to man; and whoever fails to understand it in this manner does not know what he is saying when he takes the word revelation on his lips.

· But let us continue the parable. *From the troop which occupies the front line* (it is not a group of poets and thinkers, nor are they men who have time and leisure to meditate on the things of man, nor are they men engaged with *their own* deeds and sufferings; rather, they are fighting men who are compelled to face this enemy) *comes the report* (not a theoretical system, nor an esthetic appreciation, nor a work program but a hasty and urgent report) *of the fact of this attack* (not of the well-being or ill-being of the fighting men, nor of the existence and nature of the enemy but simply of the fact: we have been attacked) *to reenforcements who are standing in readiness immediately behind the front line* (not to a group of journalists or other battlefield loafers but to a troop not unlike the men of the first line which is destined to engage the enemy and appointed to give battle). The group whom the enemy has already attacked are the prophets and apostles; and their report to the other group which is standing behind the front line prepared to reenforce them is the Holy Scripture. Whoever fails to understand these men and this book in such a manner does not have a truly realistic understanding of them.

We bring the parable to a close. *The arrival of their report is to those standing in the rear a quite self-evident signal* (a discussion of the *practical* importance of this report is quite excluded) *of the necessity* (not of a *possibility* but of the necessity which finds expression in immediate and definite commands) *to arise, take up arms, form into line, and march to the front* (all this the more quickly and energetically, the more overwhelming the superiority of the attacking enemy and the greater the danger which is threatening from the front line.)

These reenforcements whom the report from the front line has called up is the Church which hears the Holy Scripture. The moment of the call, and thus of decision, resolution, command, and obedience is the moment in which we stand: the moment of confession. We are called to hasten to the place where the prophets and apostles are making their stand. They are standing face to face with the coming GOD. They call us to their side; not for their own sake but for the sake of God. The troop which has heard them and sets out in their direction is the Church, the confessing Church. A Church which has an understanding of its existence and nature different from the one here indicated would be an uninteresting affair.

In making use of this parable, I do not lay claim to originality. It is possible to speak in an original manner on every subject in the whole wide world except this one. Of this subject it is possible only to speak faithfully, *i.e.,* exegetically. With what I have said, I merely have tried to restate how the prophets and apostles, how the Church fathers and reformers understood the testimony of the Bible, and how we ourselves must understand the Church and the confession, and thus also ourselves, if we are to remain in line with them.

For a beginning we shall pass up what will need to be said concerning the concepts of testimony and confession, and proceed to fix some propositions which have validity if, in conformity with prophets and apostles, revelation is understood to be an event of the free and sovereign activity of God toward man.

What will knowledge of revelation mean

then? Four points will be seen to be fundamental.

1. Knowledge of revelation does not always begin with clarity. It may increase in clarity; it should do so. It may, however, diminish also in clarity. But under all circumstances, it begins with certitude. Either God has spoken or He has not spoken. If He has spoken, He has done so in such a manner that it is impossible not to heed Him. Among others, the question of His existence and nature are then decided and can be answered only *a posteriori*. Doubt and despair, human unbelief, and even a sea of uncertainties on our part, will not be able to change the certitude of His presence. Revelation is this divine presence. Innumerable human questions may arise in the face of this divine presence. But every one is related to the answer which has already been given in the revelation of His presence. Certitude has the first and last word, not as our certitude but as the certitude of God.

2. Knowledge of revelation may be interrupted. It may even cease altogether. It may be bartered away for false knowledge and vain revelation. But, wherever it takes place, it possesses the character of singularity (Ein-

maligkeit). As a man can have only one father; as he is able to look at one time with his eyes into the eyes of only one other man; as he can hear with his two ears the word of only one man at one and the same time; as he is born only once and dies but once—so he can believe and know only one revelation. It is quite possible to place alongside each other, and compare a multiplicity of religions, but not a multiplicity of revelations. Whoever says revelation says one single revelation which has happened once and for all, irrevocably and unrepeatedly. As certainly as God is one. Possibility vanishes before His reality, and probability disappears before His truth. Before His face, evasion, either to the right or to the left, is impossible. In His presence there is no room left for choice, but only for decision, and always and only for decision.

3. Knowledge of revelation may be surrounded and accompanied by a rich variety of human fate. It may bring with it the profoundest external and inward experiences and call forth heroic deeds in a man. It may lift to mountain tops of human joy and plunge into an abyss of human sorrow. For revelation concerns itself with man, and every one

of these things is a part of human life. But there remains—no, in the knowledge of revelation alone there emerges and comes to the surface the world-wide difference existing between, and separating, God and man.

It is man in his totality whom God meets in His revelation. They who would mix and confuse God and man, either in understanding man to be himself God or in looking upon God as the profoundest part of man's nature or as man's highest ideal, certainly never have seen that battlefield, nor have they heard the report from the battlefield of prophets and apostles. He who understands the meeting of God and man which takes place in revelation to be a union or fusion of these two principals of revelation, must be very much of a stranger in our world, a very untroubled spectator of our troubled affairs; or he must be passionately enamored with his own fate, activity, and suffering, and he must have heard little or nothing of the action of the opponent who confronts in his sovereign superiority man's fate and existence. There is not another moment in time, not another place in all the world, which offers less opportunity for the temptation of mixing and fusing man and God

than where God and man really find each other:
in God's revelation.

4. Knowledge of revelation can and must
mean, then, a knowledge of the far away,
strange, and holy God. It prohibits the use-
less and dangerous thought that, in meeting
God, man can appear and cooperate as God's
partner, as if he were filled and endowed with
a capacity and good will for God. Knowledge
of revelation means always an acknowledge-
ment of the miracle by reason of which this
meeting takes place. Their meeting is acknowledged to be occasioned by God's grace,
mercy, and condescension. These very words,
however, distinctly affirm revelation to be a
real relation between God and man, a relation
the foundation of which is laid in Him from
whom it possesses and derives its strength and
permanence. It means that it is not founded
on the ambiguous truth of our human nature,
reason, or love. It is founded, however, on
the free decision of the eternal and unchange-
able God. The man to whom this relation
still persists to be a question, or the man who
would dare to deny it, would not have before
his eyes *God's* attack, divine *action*. Knowledge of revelation does not mean an abstract

knowledge of a God confronting an abstract man. Rather, it is a concrete knowledge of *the* God who has sought man and meets him in his *concrete* situation and finds him there. Revelation is a concrete knowledge of God and man in the event brought about by the initiative of a sovereign God. This is what constitutes the glory of God: where the infinite difference between God and man becomes manifest, there indeed it becomes manifest also that man belongs to God not because he is capable of God, not because he has sought and found him, but because it is God's gracious will to make man His own.

We have spoken of revelation. We could not possibly speak of it without anticipating the decisive factors in the problem of the nature and content of revelation. Why that certitude? Why that singularity (Einmaligkeit)? Why the unheard-of separation and relation between God and man which revelation effects? For the reason that revelation—that which came to prophets and apostles as revelation— is nothing less than God Himself. For this reason it is a mystery, *i.e.,* a reality the possibility of which resides absolutely within itself; and therefore, also, we shall never, no, not in all eternity, be able to understand, derive, and substantiate it except out of itself. God is of and through Himself. We, likewise, are able to meditate on revelation only if our thinking begins with revelation when it has spoken for itself. And, therefore, it is authority, *i.e.,* it is a truth which cannot be measured by the rule of any other truth beside it, however profound and valid that truth may appear to be. Rather, it is a truth which decides, and continues to decide what may be true. It is a truth then with whose acknowledgment every truth must make its beginning; and without its acknowledgment even profoundest truth is deception and a lie. And for the reason that revelation is God Himself, it is the court of last appeal for man—grace to him who accepts its verdict of condemnation as being God's right, condemnation to him who will not receive this grace, but who asserts, and insists upon, his rights as a man in opposition to it.

Because revelation is God Himself! Twice the Christian Church was compelled to contend for the victory of this knowledge. The first time it was in the fourth century when the doctrine of the Trinity was at stake, *i.e.,* the acknowledgment of the essential deity of

Jesus Christ and the Holy Spirit. In consummating this acknowledgment in a dogma, the Church gave expression to this: exactly in believing revelation, the Church believes God Himself; and she believes God Himself by believing revelation. This is what the Subordination and Modalist antitrinitarians of every age have never understood and never will understand. It was well and necessary that the Church did not permit itself to be led into error by their arguments.

The second battle for this same truth was fought in the sixteenth century, when the Reformation doctrine of free grace was at stake. The reformers were concerned about a right understanding of the justification of the sinner. They contended that it was an act in which the gift which is bestowed on the sinner is identical with the Giver of the gift, with His feelings, disposition, and dealings with that man, with the deed of God in which He gives and grants Himself freely to us: Immanuel. Jesus Christ is and remains our only justification; therefore, it can be ours only by faith in Him. This is what medieval Roman Catholicism did not yet understand and what modernistic Protestantism of every hue and shade proceeded and persists to forget. The Reformation doctrine, in its Lutheran as well as in its Calvinistic form, says with the same simplicity as did the Council of Nicæa: God Himself is the content of His revelation.

It is quite possible that the battle has entered its third stage today. Throughout the world, the Church is concerned today with the problem of the secularization of the modern man. It would perhaps be more profitable if the Church were at least to begin to become concerned with the problem of its own secularization. Secularism surely reigns where interest in divine revelation has been lost or bartered away for the interests of man. Is it unjust to say that knowledge of divine revelation has been forgotten where revelation is taken to be a change, an improvement, a perhaps very arbitrarily devised changed and improvement of man? Where it has been forgotton that revelation is God Himself? Where, therefore, awareness of its mystery, authority, and judgment has been lost? Where its authority and its singularity are neglected? Where awareness of the chasm between God and man, and therefore also the bridge which unites them, has been lost sight of? Is the

Church surprised that it has little or nothing to say to the modern man? Continuing on this path, it will have increasingly less to say to him. Perhaps it is high time and a matter of supreme importance for the Church to take up in all seriousness the battle for the old truth, the battle of Nicæa and of the Reformers—God's revelation is God Himself, the one, ever-present, eternal, and living God.

But whatever may be our judgment of the demands of the hour, this is the meaning, content, and dynamic of the revelation which met the biblical prophets and apostles: God Himself is here in the fact that Jesus Christ and the Holy Spirit are here. He is with us *as we are*, yes, He is Himself what we are. He has assumed our nature; He has made our sin His own, and He has made our death His. To Him who is endowed with the fulness of the divine majesty, nothing that is human is foreign. He took upon Himself our fate, our godlessness, yea, the torture of our hell. Our deepest misery is His misery also. Yes, exactly in the depths of our misery He intercedes for us, and substitutes Himself for us, warding off the wages justly due us and suffering and making restitution what we could not suffer and where we could not make restitution. He Himself, Jesus Christ, who has suffered the death of a sinner and sits at the right hand of the Father, is our advocate. He Himself, the Holy Spirit, who with groanings that cannot be uttered, makes intercession for us who do not know what we should pray. This is what revelation means, this is its content and dynamic: Reconciliation has been made and accomplished. Reconciliation is not a truth which revelation makes known to us; reconciliation is the truth of God Himself who grants Himself freely to us in His revelation. God, who is the mighty, holy, and eternal God, gave Himself to us, who are so impotent, so unholy, and mortal. Revelation is reconciliation, as certainly as it is God Himself: God with us; God beside us, and chiefly and decisively, God for us.

Whatever else it may be possible to say about that nature and content of revelation is dependent on this fact. Call it an act of the divine sovereignty by which God declares, enforces, and maintains Himself to be the Creator of a man who, though he has abused and lost his freedom, nevertheless belongs to Him; the Creator of a world which, though it has become an enigma to this man, belongs to God, nevertheless. Call revelation an act of forgiveness in which God accepts this man in spite of his sin as one who is right for Him and so calls him His child out of pure mercy, *i.e.,* for the sake of his divine righteousness. Call it an act of sanctification in which God gives man His commandment and calls him to Himself, lays claim to him for Himself, and dignifies him who is without capacity and good-will for God, that he might serve Him, live and suffer for Him, and love and praise Him. Call it an act of promise by which God gives to this man and to his world a hope and an outlook and expectation of His coming reign and kingdom, of redemption, joy, and peace in His kingdom, in which God will wipe away all tears from their eyes and death shall be no more, neither mourning, nor crying, nor pain: for the first things are passed away.

None of these things are wanting in the revelation which has come to the prophets and apostles. They were right in giving it all these names and definitions. They met in it the sovereign will of the Creator, the Reconciler, and of the Redeemer. But let us not forget that they were met first and foremost

with the sovereign will of God the Reconciler;
first and foremost with Jesus Christ, the Word
of God which has come to sinners; and first
and foremost with the Holy Spirit through
whom sinners are called to repentance. The
second article of the Creed does not occupy
its central place by sheer accident. Primarily
and chiefly, it must be accepted as valid truth:
God for us! Not something divine, not something akin to God, or something coming from
God. No, God Himself. Since it has pleased
God to grant us nothing less than Himself, we
are compelled to confess: So great must be our
misery that nothing less than God Himself was
able to help us. Or, so great is God's love for us
that He refused to give us anything less than
Himself. We need to thank Him that He did
just what He did. This is revelation: the event
of God's sovereign initiative. That it is an
event, we are told by the biblical witnesses. If
they are right in what they report, then it is
indeed the event of all events. Descartes is
wrong, then, when he says: Cogito, ergo sum.
For by the reason of this revelation, we are less
certain of our own existence than of God's
existence for us.

THE CHURCH

As we begin our inquiry into the nature of the Church, it seems advisable to set forth, and reject, two errors.

The Church is not divine revelation institutionalized. It is not an organization into whose possession, disposition, and administration God has resigned His will and truth and grace in the form of a definite sum of supernatural powers, insights, and virtues. It is knowledge peculiar to the Church that God's will is the will of a sovereign Lord who does not share his glory with man. The Church is aware that the truth of God is not an object—not even a supernatural object—but the eternal subject which makes itself known to us in a mystery only, and only to faith. And it is peculiar to the Church that it adores the grace of God in the person of Jesus Christ, *i.e.,* a grace so original in character and function that it excludes every thought of cooperation, either of man or any other creature. The Church understands it therefore to be the sovereign act of the Holy Spirit. The Church is not a human way of salvation nor an apparatus for man's salvation with which God identified His own kingdom. We have drawn a line of demarcation against the error of the Roman Catholic Church.

But neither is the Church a voluntary association for the cultivation of impressions, experiences, and impulses which men may have received from divine revelation and by reason of which they have formed definite convictions, condensed them into definite resolutions, rules, and customs of life and made them the center of their piety and morals. The Church is not the result of human election, decision, and disposition toward divine revelation. It arises from the election, decision, and disposition of God toward man. In revelation they have become an event. There God meets men and communicates Himself to men. Men are not gathered into, nor preserved as, the Church by an agreement in sentiments, convictions, and resolutions. Rather, it is the one God, one Christ, one Spirit, one baptism, one faith. The Church is not a religious society. We reject the error of modernistic Protestantism.

Both errors have two misconceptions in common. They magnify the Church while at the same time minimizing it. They magnify it by placing too great a trust in man, and they minimize it by trusting God too little. In the Church, man is neither a vessel of supernatural authority, insight, and power, as Roman Catholicism teaches, nor is he the free religious personality of modernistic Protestantism. And in the Church, God is neither the supernatural being which becomes actual here and there, by means of sacred channels, an object of man's contemplation and enjoyment, nor is He something like an *elan vital* of nature or history to which a specific aptitude and experience provides access and over which man may, after all, gain control in the form of special convictions and attitudes, as a virtuoso has control over his instrument.

Rather, the constitution and preservation of the Church rests in this, that man hears God. This is what makes it truly great and truly little. In the Church man hears God because He has spoken, and he gives ear to what God has spoken. The Church exists wherever this is done, even if it consists of only two or three persons. Even if these two or three people do not belong to select society or average respectability but to the scum of the earth. Even if these two or three people are quite disheartened and perplexed as they face the question what they ought to do now about what they have heard. Even if they should not exert any influence and have no large significance in the environment and in the society in which they live.

The Church will gain true courage and genuine significance whenever and wherever it is firmly resolved to resign the false courage and counterfeit significance—the courage of large numbers, of moral qualities, of activistic programs, of effect on and appreciation from those without—with the intent of putting its sole confidence in what founds and preserves it as it unites in lending an open ear to what God has spoken.

Evangelism and cultivation of fellowship may be very desirable. We may well rejoice that the question of the form of our divine service has become an open question again; that the problem of ecclesiastical law does not suffer the neglect today to which it has been exposed so long; that theology everywhere is beginning to awaken in a new endeavor to

be what its name implies. The consciousness
of the political and social responsibility of
the Church which has come to life with the
beginning of our century almost everywhere
where our evangelical faith is confessed, may
be forced to change its form, but under no
condition must it go to sleep again. It is
necessary that the Church face, and face ever
anew, the questions which the modern development of psychology and education pro-
pose to it, What is pastoral care? What is
Christian education? And the Church must
not attempt to escape the necessity of remembering and continually remembering what the
missionary activities in its midst are saying:
A world engulfed in a sea of misery is waiting
—not for the Church but—to become Church
itself. It is waiting to hear because God has
spoken. It is waiting to hear what God has
spoken.

But after affirming all these tasks, we shall
be compelled to return—and in taking these
tasks seriously we shall inevitably and unceas-
ingly be compelled to return—to the beginning,
not this or that good, however necessary it
may be, but in all these efforts this one thing
makes the Church a genuine church, namely,

that man hears God because God has spoken
and lends an ear to what He has spoken. And
where this is not done, where perhaps only a
sacred apparatus is functioning or where the
interests of a religious association are substituted, where in one form or another too much
confidence is placed in man, and God is trusted
too little, there we deny the existence of a
Church. It is not a Church even if it draws
multitudes to its bosom and wins the support
of the most outstanding individuals; even if it
displays a rich variety of life and wins the profoundest respect of state and society.

At different points of our modern world we
find ourselves in a promising, but also dangerous, situation. From many an unexpected
quarter inquiry is made about the nature
and message of the Church. Here and there
churchliness is on the point of becoming fash-
ionable again. We do not know, nor ought
we to care, whither this development will lead.
It is not our business either to foster or to ham-
per it. But we need to be aware that today
in particular the question has become decisive
if the Church will become and be at the place
where the one thing is done that makes it and
preserves it as a Church. Without it we shall

surely win victories; but they will soon prove
to be grave defeats. And with equal certainty,
real victories which may today come suddenly
within its grasp will escape it.

The path of the Church is remarkably narrow indeed. It is so for the reason that in
thinking of the Church we are thinking, almost with a sort of natural necessity, either
in terms of Roman Catholicism or modernistic Protestantism, or, alternating between
the errors of the one or the other, we develop
a combination and synthesis of them. The only
method of escape out of this labyrinth is and
can be the method of the Holy Spirit and of
faith.

In defining man's lending his ear to God
as being the decisive moment of the Church,
we surely emphasize also its humanity, its
worldliness, and its profane character. And
we state it to be not a mere blemish when we
say that the very existence, form, and message
of the Church shares in the darkness of the
man who has lost God and who remains lost
if God does not recover him. In fact, the
Church participates to an even fuller extent
in the world's darkness and is even more profane than the rest of the world surrounding

it. For the man who hears God—in fact, he alone—is aware of his profane character. It is essential to the Church that nothing human is foreign to it. It is always and everywhere the Church of man, a Church of particular ages and peoples, and languages and cultures. But beyond these, its sympathy, yes, its solidarity with the world is most complete where it seems to differ most sharply from the world: *e.g.,* the world of politics, of science, or of art: in the Church the boundaries of humanity are respected and guarded. The Church does not worship idols. It does not cultivate ideologies. In the Church man must needs have a very sober view and understanding of himself. He sees his finitude and nakedness, his limitations and solitariness. The world was not always grateful to the Church for ignoring its idols. It is a well-known fact that there were times when the world persecuted the Church for this reason. Perhaps the Church would suffer persecution again, if it would clearly set forth its distinctiveness from the world by ignoring its idols.

But let it not be overlooked, in that which really makes it differ from the world, the Church is even more worldly than the world,

more humanistic than the humanists. In it, it
comes nearer to the real meaning of every human tragedy-comedy which as an attempt on
one man's part to help himself could be genuine
only if it confines itself within its natural limitations by waiving all religious pomp and
claims. The world's secret is the non-existence
of its gods. At the price of floods of tears
and blood, the world keeps denying its secret
and seeks to populate nature and history with
its idols. The deep reason of its unrest is its
refusal to confess its profane character. The
Church is aware of this secret of the world.
It must not permit itself to be befuddled by
reproaches and accusations. Just so it is truly
loyal to the world.

But this faithfulness of the Church to the
world is after all possible only as the reverse side
of an entirely different loyalty. The Church
is in existence where man hears God. Not
gods, not something divine, but God. God is
not a power or a truth, or even a being which
man can discover by himself in order to clothe
it with the title of deity. On the contrary, God
is He who became known to man as his real
Lord by meeting Him by his initiative in judgment, forgiveness, sanctification, and promise:

by revealing himself. That this has happened
we are told by apostles and phophets. Who
else should have told us? To be sure, many
books bring us records of gods and things
divine; but of God Himself this book alone.
Where the voice of those was heard who stood
in expectation and remembrance of Jesus
Christ, the Church came into existence: et in
hanc petram ædificabo ecelesiam meam. *Where
the Scriptures speak*—and through the Scriptures God Himself in the language of His
mighty deeds—*and where man hears*—hears
God Himself in the word of his witnesses—
*there the Church comes into existence and
exists*. We deny the existence of the Church
apart from this relationship.

In this relationship it is begotten and born
to the world. It is nourished by it. In it,
it has room to move and air to breathe. This
relationship possesses the peculiar character
of revelation itself, and the Church does not
acknowledge the existence of any compensa-
tory substitute for it. It is the sole riches of
the Church. But it is the Church's life-con-
dition also, and its neglect must result in its
immediate plunge into an abyss of nothingness.
It is to the Church that the gospel, with its

mysterious mark of excellence over the state, over every school of philosophy, over conservative as well as revolutionary movements, gives to humanity's history its manifold and constantly changing forms. But it is also very simply the law of the Church to which it must cling. In its exposition and obedience it must continually exercise itself if it is to remain— or become again—Church.

Note well the relationship between the Holy Scriptures and the Church, and the foundation of the Church on this rock of Peter, is at no time anything less than a revelatory event, *i.e.,* the eternal word and its Holy Spirit in action. For this reason, the testimony of the prophets and apostles which is the means of this action, as a tool in God's hands as it were, stands always sovereign, *above* the Church and its teachers and preachers, its dogmas, customs, and institutions. These latter are bound to the former while the former is not bound to the latter. The Scriptures govern the Church, and not the Church the Scriptures.

But note well: the Scriptures as a tool in *God's* hands. For they are only human testimony of divine revelation. Therefore, the Scriptures, so far as God elects to speak at

this moment and under these circumstances
to these people through these men and deter-
mines so to build His Church; the Scriptures
which at times to many or to all is almost, if
not actually, a sealed book; the Scriptures
which speak to us perhaps in only relatively
small portions as our contemporary; the Scriptures from which the word of God strikes us
always as a flash of lightning out of dark
clouds—but which as a whole demand our
constant attention because as a whole their
origin and meaning bear witness of divine
revelation and for this reason are rightfully
called "Holy" Scriptures, canon of the Church,
by which the Church is constantly measured
and which it is the Church's duty constantly to
search and humbly to expound.

This is the other, and the genuine and
original faithfulness which is peculiar to the
Church. This is its faithfulness to God. For
faithfulness to God means for the Church,
simply and concretely, faithfulness to this
book. In this faithfulness, the Church's faithfulness to the world is rooted. It makes the
Church a place where sobriety reigns and therefore a place of a genuinely worldly character.
The question if and how the Church can

exist, depend simply and concretely on the other questions whether the Church is capable of putting its confidence in this book, and therefore feels constrained to obey it. In such trust and obedience consists what was previously called the method of the Holy Spirit and of faith. Study the history of the Church! Did it ever consist in anything else? And whoever is concerned about what the world thinks of the Church ought to become aware of the fact that the world is interested in only one question about the Church: Does the Church still dare, and dare ever and ever again, to cling simply and concretely to the method of the Holy Spirit and faith? The Church which dared to do so always overcame the kingdoms of this world—secretly or openly. But the Church gained this mastery only where it did not seek it. For in order to make this method effective, the last security of Roman Catholic and modernistic clericalism must be sacrificed.

If it is true that hearing the word of God, submission to it, and being bound by it constitutes the concrete order of life for the Church —if it is true that the Church comes to life, always and ever, by the word of apostles and prophets as it calls us to join their ranks in order that with them we may become face to face with the initiative of God and with them become witnesses of revelation and hearers of his word—then it is also true that life in the Church, yes the life of the Church itself, *must* be humility and service.

In more than one instance the New Testament gives to those who desire to listen to God and to the word of his prophets and apostles as its foremost direction the admonition to *tapeinophrosune*. It signifies thinking in submissive abasement before God and men. There is no danger that a spirit of domination will die out either in public or private life. The state represents sovereignty, culture means dominion, and even the best and purest development of human nature is a will-to-rule. There is not one among us who does not have a share in some such rule, and there is none who does not somehow strive for it. And the rule of men is always sinful and perverse. In spite of this insight, the Church has always acknowledged—also in this respect, obedient to the Scriptures—that this sinful and perverse government among men is a necessary divine order to restrain its equally sinful and perverse freedom.

Just as definitely, however, the Church has found its calling to consist in something else than in the establishment and maintenance of such a rule. It will give to Cæsar what is Cæsar's, but it can never give its unconditional sanction to any such form of mastery, to any form of the state or trend of culture. It cannot join hands with any of them for better or worse. It is in no wise its office to undergird man and aid his ascendancy. Where it does affirm man's rule over men it will do so in reverence of the hidden intent of God and not of the only-too-patent plans of man. It will have regard for the patience and wisdom of God who knows to set bounds to sin even by sin itself. But for the sake of God and man, it will keep its hands free for its own peculiar task. The sign which it is called to erect is a sign other than the sign of dominion. For this reason, it will not conceive its task to be the establishment of a rule of its own. It will not proceed to build a city of God in opposition to the cities of the world, a realm of the pious against the realm of the godless, an island of the righteous and blessed in the midst of the sea of wickedness. Its very sympathy and solidarity will prevent its doing so.

And neither will the Church fail to appreciate that of all tyrannies, religious tyranny, the rule over the consciences of men, in matters of minor or major importance, in the name of God, carried through by external or spiritual means, is its most fearful, yes, its most accursed form. After having kept its hands clean of the secular forms of world tyrannies, it must now become a victim of this temptation. The sign which the Church must erect—or rather, the sign under which the Church has been placed from its very inception reads: Service, and not rule!

But, again, we need to be careful lest we change service to hidden tyranny. The concept service is not unknown outside of the Church. Did not the most ambitious men and the most efficient tyrannies advertise themselves as having come to serve? Let the Church beware lest it join their ranks. And the danger is especially great in days when the Church awakens to a new self-consciousness and a new will-to-live. Where we are bent on serving according to our own good judgment and under rules of our making, we are not rendering true service. Dostoievski's grand inquisitor meant well with God and man, but he

wanted to serve God and man with his own
good intentions.. For this reason, his service
became the most subtle kind of tyranny.
Where an arbitrarily designed plan and way
of salvation, based on arbitrary notions of God
and man, holds sway, intentions may be ever
so good and pious; but true service to God and
man is not rendered there. Neither can there
be a true Church. We may rest assured: the
arbitrary character of such plans and ways
will always betray itself in that too little confidence is placed in God and too much in man.

The appeal to God's goodness and man's
godly nature—in their generally accepted
meaning—has never given serious consideration to the lost condition of man, nor to the
grace of God. But it will make room for all
manner of syntheses between God and man.
Their name, however, is not Christ; they are
humanity and infused grace. For man's un-
controlled and arbitrary reflection on God and
man and salvation has always arrived at the
conclusion that *much* indeed, but not *everything,* depends on Christ. In the last analysis,
we are not in such bitter need of him, anyway.
It is neither immoral nor is it a character blemish to arrive at this thought. No other thought

in all the world lies so near at hand. Nothing comes easier to us than to think that nature is not without grace and grace is in a way nature, too. And it is quite possible to make it a Christian principle and carry it into actual practice. The teachers and practitioners of this arbitrariness have never yet failed to clothe their notions with the glorious garment of pure humility and charitable service. But arbitrariness has never begotten anything else than a bastard Church: clericalism. Clericalism is the rule of those who claim to have gained knowledge of a unity of nature and grace. There is no tyranny more terrible than such an one. For in its every form it is nothing less than the rule of anti-Christ.

Humility and service, the signs under which the Church has been placed, must be radically divorced from the humility and service of clericalism, if they are to indicate to us the presence of the Church. The Church possesses no independent knowledge. It lives from what it has been told. The Church does not live an arbitrary life, however well meant it may be. It lives in obedience. The Church has, therefore, no plans and programs of its own. It is ever alert to hear commands. The Church

does not have above it a *theme,* but a *Lord,* and
messengers who inform it of His will.   The
Church is not a society of pious people; it is
the Church of Jesus Christ.   It is not itself
Jesus Christ, but it believes in Him.   It is the
body of which He is the Head.   It cannot be
otherwise, since the axiom of its foundation
has called it to join the ranks of the apostles
and prophets.   And where these stand, eye
to eye with God in action, the spirit of arbitrary service is excluded not only in its public
but also in its hidden form.   *There* man enters
a school, and his activity consists in repeating
what he is told.   No one speaks there of a fusion of God and man and of nature and grace.
All that is known there is Jesus Christ who has
overcome their contradiction.   And this school
proclaims this Lord, and Him alone.   For
He desires to be proclaimed because no man
can ever hear enough of Him and there is not
a man who ought not hear of Him.

THEOLOGY

Of all the sciences which stir the head and heart, theology is the fairest. It is closest to human reality and gives us the clearest view of the truth after which all science quests. It best illustrates the time-honored and profound word: "Fakultaet." It is a landscape, like the landscape of Umbria or Tuscany, in which distant perspectives are always clear. Theology is a masterpiece, as well-planned and yet as bizarre as the cathedrals of Cologne and Milan. What a miserable lot of theologians —and what miserable periods there have been in the history of theology—when they have not realized this!

But of all the sciences there is none which is so beset with difficulties, none which is so beset with dangers, as theology! In no other science is it so easy to be caught in despair, or, what is worse, to end in arrogant overconfidence. It is the science which is most easily diffused or petrified, and which can become its own worst caricature. Is there a science that can be so monstrous and so boresome as theology? That man would hardly be a theologian who had never shrunk from its terrible precipice, or had ceased to be afraid of its dangers.

But, both are true. And both have their basis in the fact that theology has its own peculiar nature, its own necessity for being, its own possibility to exist, its own task, and its own effects. It does not need to justify itself; it cannot justify itself; and it should not desire to do so. Theology is the freest and yet the most restricted of all the sciences. All the questions regarding its justification are simply answered by calling attention to the Church and the divine revelation upon which the Church was founded. This is the only answer theology can hope to give, and with this one answer theology has removed all its claims to an independent justification.

This is certainly a royal assumption whereupon theology rests. It is an assumption whereby even the most casual theological arguments, if they are truly theological, receive an ardor and a glory that is incomparable.

But this assumption of theology cannot be exhibited as the natural scientist exhibits his phenomena, nor as the historian does his facts, nor as the philosopher, or the mathematician, does his axioms, nor as the lawyer, or the sociologist, does his sociological possibilities and necessities, upon which all of these build their research and teaching. Theology cannot even mark the boundary of its problem, nor mark the bounds of its research and its teaching in a general, or exact, way so that it might make certain its province among the other sciences, and thereby make its assumption valid, at least in some visible and tangible way.

Theology's essential hypothesis, or axiom, is revelation, which is God's own act done in His Word and through His Spirit. How shall this axiom be exhibited or determined? It cannot be done directly, but indirectly. Not positively but negatively. Not by setting it a bound among other sciences. Theology would be falsified or misinterpreted, betrayed or given up, if it sought to make its fundamental assumption or axiom a direct and tangible exhibit. Theology would have ceased to be theology, if it sought to, or could, justify itself.

It has always been forsaken by its guardian angels above, every time it has sought to take this way.

For example, is there anything more hopeless than the attempt that has been made in the last two hundred years with ever-increasing enthusiasm to create a systematic link-up, or synthesis, or even a discriminate relationship, between the realms of theology and philosophy? Has there been one reputable philosopher who has paid the least attention to the work which the theologians have attempted in this direction? Has it not become apparent that the anxiety and uncertainty with which we pursued this course only reminded us that we can pursue this course only with an uneasy conscience? Theology can become noticed by philosophy only after that moment when it no longer seeks to be interesting. Its relation to philosophy can become positive and fruitful only after it resolutely refuses to be itself a philosophy and refuses to demonstrate and base its existence upon a principle with, or alongside of, philosophy.

And this is true of the relation between theology and all other sciences. As the revelation of God and the Church exist in fact—revelation existing in and of itself, and the Church upon revelation—so theology must and can only exist in fact. Theology must prove its own existence, its possibility to exist, and its necessity for existence *simply by existing!* It must prove the justification of its confidence in its fundamental assumption by simply trusting it, and out of that confidence it thinks and speaks! Theology dares, dares to be itself, and dares to work its own way! All doubt and all conceited pride, all the boresomeness, and all the monstrosity of theology, have their basis in the fact that theology has not dared to be itself. If it would not be ashamed of itself, it would not need to be ashamed. Theology must not defend itself—only then will it be immune from attack. Let theology avoid all interests but its own, then it will not be isolated. It is isolated so long as it is afraid that it will be isolated.

The task which is laid upon theology, and which it should and can fulfill is its service in the Church, to the Lord of the Church. It has its definite function in the Church's liturgy, that is, in the various phases of the Church's expression: In every reverent proclamation of the gospel, or in every proclaiming reverence,

in which the Church listens and attends to God.
Theology does not exist in a vacuum, nor in
any arbitrarily selected field, but in that province between baptism and communion, in the
realm between the Scriptures and their exposition and proclamation. Theology is like all
other functions of the Church, uniquely based
upon the fact that God has spoken to men and
that men may hear His word through grace.
Theology is an act of repentant humility, which
is presented to men through this fact. This
act exists in the fact that in theology the
Church seeks again and again to examine
itself critically as it asks itself what it means
and implies to be a Church among men.

But the Church is an aggregation of humans,
even fallible, erring, sinful people. Nothing
is more self-evident than that the Church is
constantly recreated from age to age, and yet
it *is* Church. The Church, too, lives under the
judgment of God, as does the world. So, it
cannot be otherwise but that the Church must
critically examine itself, not according to its
own wishes or standards but according to the
standard that is identical with its basis of existence, which is God's revelation, which, concretely, is the Holy Scriptures. It is this con-

stant and ever-recurring necessity and demand
for self-examination of the Church by the
standard of the divine Word which is the peculiar function of theology in the Church.

On the basis of these principles we may draw
a few necessary conclusions:

1. Theology cannot of itself select the truth
which it must make valid in the Church. It
must make this truth valid, not because that
truth is the most comprehensible, or possible,
nor because it is the most practical. All this
smacks of *chosen* truth, and, therefore, cannot
come into consideration here, but this truth
must be made valid because it *is* already selected, not *by* theology but *for* theology. This
truth is one already chosen because it *is* valid.
Wherever theology has desired to assume the
selection of truth, it still has selected human
disputable truth; it has given up its true nature. I have called theology the freest and yet
the most restricted science. Its freedom is the
freedom of God. Is there a more sovereign
act than the act of theological thinking, the
act of recognition and validation of the Word
of God as the Word of the God of heaven on
earth, the Lord of life and death? Now, this
freedom is found only in the strictest loyalty

to the Word of God. Even the most "religious" or "pious" freedom outside this loyalty
would be mere libertinism and not true theological freedom.

2. Theology, therefore, cannot appear as
though it were a branch and an application of
a historical science which can be carried on
under the ensign of an idealism today, and
under the ensign of a positivism tomorrow, and
the day after tomorrow under the ensign of
skepticism. Certainly, the original sources
and documents of revelation are monuments
of human history. Certainly, the investigation
of revelation's documents must always be
historical, therefore, always historico-critical.
And it is to be assumed that every historical
critic will have a certain philosophical bias
either idealistic, positivistic, or skeptical toward
his materials, *i.e.*, the Bible, the dogmas of the
fourth and fifth centuries, and the Reformation.

But it makes quite a difference whether a
man expects to discover, (by way of these presuppositions) independent, so-called "historical truth" of the most supreme "value," or
whether he expects to find God's Word in the
documents of the Church. It is an altogether

different matter whether a man in the pursuit of this investigation and interpretation relies ultimately upon *himself* as an idealist, positivist, or skeptic, or whether he relies upon himself as an obedient *hearer of the Word*. It makes quite a difference whether a man speculates as an historian, as a responsible and integral member of the Church, or, whether he speculates as an independent idealist, positivist, or skeptic. The historical technique and method will not be of a different kind in either case, but the problems, the historical attitudes, the interests, and, ultimately, the whole meaning and interpretation of history will be investigated and interpreted differently. Whoever makes this "historical truth" out of his own world-outlook, whoever identifies it with the truth of God, may become a great historian, but he will not be able to speak with authority, or with good sense as an historical *theologian*.

3. Theology cannot appear as a quest for truth or a philosophy of general truth. So far as theology bows to the truth of revelation, it understands that the different world views which are designated "truth" are, at best, only relative, tentative, and limited truth. It is not, however, the task of theology to place it-

self, so to speak, over or between the antithesis between God's revelation and human
reason and its world views, so as to establish
a relation between these two, to present revelation as reason, or reason as revelation, and
thereby bring them into one system.

It is this which the "gnosis" of every age
and type have attempted again and again.
"Gnosis" means to see and think of revelation
and reason, God and man, grace and nature
as united from God's standpoint. As a result,
in every case, "gnosis" has misunderstood both.
Theology is not "gnosis." Theology does not
usurp God's standpoint. Theology listens to
God's revelation and understands revelation's
relation to human reason to be a meeting of
two things, as a conversation in which the former speaks and the latter listens, in which
grace gives and nature receives, in which God
reigns and man obeys. Theology recognizes
true human truth there, and only there, where
God's truth is spoken to man.

4. Theology is not reconciliation of man with
God. Nor is it the Chuich, nor the sacraments,
nor the sermon, nor the Church's works of
charity. This reconciliation of man with God
is God, it is that God who deals with us in

Jesus Christ. Theology is a human and not the divine work. Theology is service to the Word and is not itself the Word of God. This must be said very emphatically, because men always try to, and should, discredit theology, because it is only theory and not practice, intellectualism and not life, only abstraction and not reality. Certainly, theology is not everything, not even in the life of the Church, much less in the relation between God and man.

Theology is, as has already been stated, a function in the liturgy of the Church. One had better take caution what he does, when he neglects theology, or takes it less seriously and thereby practically eliminates it, because it has only this one function. Of all the functions of the Church's liturgy none is to be dispensed with if the Church is to be kept totally intact. And it is quite in order to say very emphatically today, that it is precisely this function, that of theology, this critical self-examination of the Church regarding its reason for existence and its origin is not to be eliminated. Try to carry on your practice without a theory! Go on, praise "life" at the expense of intellectual work, knowledge, or creed! Worship "reality" and despise *truth!* It will very quickly become evi-

dent that the practical things are not all there
is to it; it is only human endeavor, and yet, in
its own autonomous nature it is not a worthy
human endeavor. Where such a path leads
can be illustrated today before our very eyes,
and concerning which the Churches of all coun-
tries have every reason to fundamentally re-
think themselves. A Church without an
orderly theology must sooner or later become
a pagan church.

But what is theology? Let us now attempt
to give a positive answer to this question.

The task of theology consists in again and
again reminding the people in the Church, both
preachers and congregations, that the life and
work of the Church are under the authority of
the gospel and the law, that God should be
heard. It has also to carefully examine how
God is spoken of in this instance, what men
mean by "God" in that instance, and what is
presented as God's will and work. It has to
be a watchman so as to carefully observe that
constant threatening and invasive error to
which the life of the Church is in danger, because it is composed of fallible, erring, sinful
people. Theology must watch that particular
theological falsity which alienates the Church

from its true nature, and makes it into a "salt without any savor" if it should gain control of the Church. This theological falsity is that relative truth which sets itself up as absolute in place of the truth of God in revelation. Against this falsity, theology has to summon itself to constant critical examination and retracing of steps. It must exhort preachers and Churches to a life of obedience.

Where theology does this task, there it finds its obligation first, last, and always in an exegesis, or interpretation of the Old and New Testaments. The Church trusts and obeys revelation, wherever it knows it. It knows it when it knows its biblical witness. To know means to understand. Therefore, preaching, that decisive function of the Church, must consist in an exposition of the divine text, in a proper guidance to its understanding. In respect to this task, theology with its exegesis must precede the preacher and stand always by his side. Theological exegesis is an historico-grammatical task, as any other, except that the theological exegesis must not allow his philosophical *Weltanschauung* (world view) to determine the meaning of the text, but he must wait upon the text to yield its witness to

revelation, to which he must subordinate himself. In the hopeful expectation—that is all
that may be said here. That he should recognize the witness and make a rational explanation of it is not in his power.

Revelation speaks, even in the Bible, only
when and where God wills it. The peculiarity
of theological exegesis can be reduced finally
to this expectancy and this respect, this attentiveness and open-mindedness which corresponds to this expectancy. In this expectancy,
the theological exegete will not be without the
guide whereby the original—mark well, the
original!—meaning of the text will not escape
him. The Bible was read and interpreted at
the hands of the Church fathers, the reformers,
and countless exegetes in this fashion, so that
it was to them a Book of Witness, and thereby
it was revelation itself, and an ever-new revelation. In their footsteps and after their example the Bible must be read and interpreted
by theology in the future.

But the preaching of the Church must not
be confined to the task of merely interpreting
the witness and word of the prophets and apostles, spoken and written thousands of years
ago. In the fact that this witness and word

have been translated into another language, and still more in that different words, concepts, and phrases are substituted for the original text, and, even more, in that the words of the original text have been amplified and thus made more explicit so that the original word is made more contemporary—in the light of these facts, the preacher dares, today, to think the thoughts of the biblical witnesses after them, and, in the name of the present-day Church, to speak them as out of his own knowledge. Out of what has been heard must proceed that which must be spoken. How else could it be heard in an increasing range? Out of insight there comes of necessity a confession. This is a necessary but a precarious transition.

Does there not arise here a so-called neutral territory upon which the false idea of modern man will seek to expand? Certainly there is, and precisely for that reason theology must assume a new form in its role of watchman. This form is dogmatics, which means a critical examination of modern, relatively free formulations of concepts and new ways of thinking relative to the interpretation of the text in the proclamation of the Church.

Dogmatics must test dogma to see that

dogma corresponds to the true object. The "dogma" is the sum total of this correspondence, or harmony, concerning which the "dogmas" of the Church have reached in some (not in all) points a certain determining unity, or fixity. Dogmatics has the task of interpreting corresponding co-relation of "the dogmas." But beyond that, its task is to carry on a comprehensive investigation of the entire Church's language, concepts, phrases, and ways of thinking in the present. It must keep in living contact with biblical exegesis, and it must make critical comparison of the conclusions of older and newer interpreters, preachers, and teachers of the Church, and thereby constantly inquire after "the dogma."

Here, too, the fruit of this critical occupation does not lie in the hands of man. The dogmatical scholar is as little in the secret counsels of God as is the exegetical scholar. If he sits down before the Bible and certain absolutely necessary documents of the Church's knowledge and confession, and acts as a man upon earth—and does not somewhat slyly try to build up his pseudo-philosophical (or philosophico-religious!) system—his labor will not be entirely in vain. In dogmatics we have to do with that which is most specifically theological of all theological disciplines. We have to do with the essential core of theological science.

Now the sermon, together with the other remaining functions of the Church's liturgy, is central. It is not a discussion and not a meditation. It is an action; it is the action in which the Church serves the Word of God in that the Church and the world may hear the Word again and again. The preacher is a human being, and those who should hear the sermon are human, people of a particular time and historical situation. For that reason the whole problem of language arises. In a practical way the question arises: With what form of sermon, and with what form of service, may the Word be so presented that it may be heard by this and that person as the Word of God?

So-called "practical theology," which here injects itself, has been unjustly treated as a stepchild of theological science. It has been entrusted in faculties to those persons who were considered insignificant, or just good enough for the position. Schleiermacher was right when he called practical theology the "crown of theology."

Here is where some very fruitful and serious work might be done. But one must make it clear that right here, more than anywhere else, one has to start and end with revelation, with the Scriptures, and not with the personally achieved psychological, pedagogical, asthetical, or political assumption or premise. How, how shall we preach? Preach so that this foundation, (which is no tangible, human foundation) may be seen today, so that God Himself might become apprehensible to us poor humans and our poor human fellow-beings? In these questions there is revealed (humanly speaking) the very reason for the existence of theology, if the reason for the theology's existence is not its very existence. If theology falters and fails here, then it has secretly failed in its exegesis and its dogmatics. Upon the basis of an orderly exegesis and dogmatics, there must be an orderly science—surely, a science!—of homiletics, of catechetics (teaching), of Church conduct, and so forth! But there is no easy receipt whereby *we may win* the love of God! But here, too, there is a labor that, because it is merely human work, needs not be without fruitful result.

In conclusion, theology is not a private subject for theologians only. Nor is it a private subject for professors. Fortunately, there have always been pastors who have understood more about theology than most professors. Nor is theology a private subject of study for pastors. Fortunately, there have repeatedly been congregation members, and often whole congregations, who have pursued theology energetically while their pastors were theological infants or barbarians. Theology is a matter for the Church.

Yet, things would not go so well without pastors or professors. But the problem of theology, as the purity of the Church's task, is set before the *whole* Church. In the Church there are really no non-theologians. The concept "laymen" is one of the worst concepts in religious terminology, a concept that should be eliminated from the Christian vocabulary. So, the pseudo-professors and the pseudo-pastors are co-responsible to see to it that the theology of the professors and pastors be a good one and not a bad one. And because revelation, because the Church, in its essential nature and purpose, is a human affair, therefore we say of theology in this confident generality: Theology is a general human matter. And there are times which need theology desperately, when one can well say: Theology is, however few may be aware of it, *the* human concern and subject.

THE MINISTRY OF THE WORD OF GOD

It is self-evident that it is to be highly desired that a pastor (or as we should more truly say: a minister of the Word of God) should be a moral character and a religious personality; a man of good taste and training; a quick thinker and yet one who is full of due respect for the laws of sound human reason. He should be a man well-grounded in life's meaning and yet sincere in his understanding regarding the joy and sorrow of his environment, both near and far. He should be sincere in prayer, a disciplined worker, a perfectly natural, and yet a uniquely spiritually-minded man, a good parent, citizen, and patriot—but one with wide horizons. He should be a man whose whole heart is steeped in his own times, that is, one who is sensitive to, and experiences the needs and hopes of, the times as his very own, and takes a stand regarding them, so that he can think and speak with his contemporaries as one of them. He must be capable and ready to love every human being, and be, therefore, capable and resolved to fear no man. He must be and remain free to make a decision and to hold to his choice as he pledges and gives himself without reservation in the battle for the good.

He must have the courage to make a lone stand, but he must also possess such humility that he can take his place as a simple private among many others in the regiment of work and struggle. He must be prepared to wait patiently in quietness, as well as be prepared for the intensest activity. He must be a man of peace, as well a man of struggle, if struggle it must be. He must, by an inner necessity, be able to express equally well the fiercest seriousness, the deepest unction, as well as the most candid humor. He must be at home in his Bible and his dogmatics. He must possess an understanding of the political issues, the movies, and sport, that is, at least, to the extent of having a sympathetic understanding for them. He must be equal to good society, and yet be a peculiarly uncitizen-like creature. His heart must be with the proletariat and just for that reason he must have none of the proletarian sentiments and prejudices. He must know the atheist and pietist better than they know themselves. He must be a psychologist, trained either by scientific education or natural bent, and yet, on the contrary, he must not be psychological at all, but know how to comfort sympathetically and fervently, or reprimand in a simple and direct way.

As a pastor and watchman and teacher and preacher to sick souls, he must be well acquainted with, and bring loving care to, the immediate problems within their four walls. But he must know and understand no less the larger movement of events transpiring out in the Church and the world within the framework of which the fate of the congregation is enacted. He must always speak to the real situation, but always from an exalted position. He must speak to men, but in such a way that something more is said to them than what they might just as well say to themselves. He must know how to think, speak, and act as a priest and as a prophet and as a pastor.

Now this short list of qualifications as to what a minister of the Word should be and do could be continued much further and each qualification might be propounded and elucidated in a more interesting fashion. There are German manses upon whose walls one finds such a list of rules for pastors which has been made up into a neat tablet. It has even been put into verse and framed behind glass. And sometimes there may be seen an appropriate companion piece, ingeniously invented and produced for the benefit of the lady of the manse. It is not likely that there is even one among us who does not need, and there ought to be none who does not feel the need, of holding or having held before him, such a table of qualifications, and, according to the plumb-line of their demands, sincerely keep in mind the most important steps of pastoral progress and amendations.

Yet, I would not care to continue speaking to you today in terms of such a table of pastoral rules and regulations. In the references I have already made, the fact has certainly not remained concealed from you, that in all of the demands not a word has yet been said concerning the ministry of the Word of God, concerning the evangelical shepherd's task, in the real meaning of this office. Everything, or perhaps, most everything that has been said thus far, might be said in the same or similar

words in the necrology of an unusual, sincere,
high-minded civic official, or a wise and righteous magistrate, or of another, rather universal,
type of well-disposed friend of God and man.
Once again: it is highly to be desired that some
day men may be able to say these things of us!
Blessed is the man who succeeds in, and who
is naturally capable of, following these demands and thereby achieving a pastoral nature
which is distinguished, excellent, kindly, de-
vout, free, and courageous; a pastoral nature
which more than once has aroused among even
cultured people of our modern age a general
and heartily expressed sympathy.

But now, it is just this modern age of ours
which, in spite of such pastors' lives, has asked
the astonishing question whether the office of
the pastor has not become superfluous! What
shall we answer to this query if our summary
of pastoral qualifications—which may sketch
for us after all only the ideal picture of what
constitutes a good, and a wise, and a sincere
man—had exhausted what needs to be said concerning the ministry of the Word? Should
these qualifications—which in a particular way
are requisites in a pastor—be anything but
highly desirable, and even necessary, predi-

cates in our particular subject—the ministry of the Word of God—without which they are wanting a solid and firm foundation, even if we fulfill them to some extent?

Perhaps, we will have to speak primarily, and only, about—*this one basic subject* of all pastoral qualifications if we should really speak about the pastor, the minister of the Word of God. And does not the chief weakness of these qualifications consist in this, that they are merely demands? I do not know if Benjamin Vallotton's "Pastor Chardonnet" ever existed in real life. But I do know that Alexander Vinet existed. But how do these ideal examples, these outstanding pastoral figures, help with all their fine qualifications, if I am not "Pastor Chardonnet" or Alexander Vinet? Yes, and what would it profit me? Would I be a minister of the Word if I possessed their genuine, respectable, and cultured humanity as my own? Were they ministers of the Word just because of those things wherein they seem to be to us a living list of pastoral qualifications? Were they not ministers of the Word upon the basis of *one* factor alone which had nothing to do with the fulfilment or non-fulfilment of these external qualifications; a factor, or element, which cannot be considered as a qualification to be achieved, but which can be described only as a gift, and a being, and a reality?

Let any one of us ask another in whom we secretly admire the fulfilment of this or that previously-mentioned qualification, whether he really thinks he is a minister of the Word because he can work with the greatest variety of people so patiently and dexterously, or be so popular with children, so friendly with the poor, or that he can stand in politics so true and fearless beside the man of his choice, or express in his person such astonishing theological expertness and cultured mien.

How commonplace, how threadbare, must be the virtues of such a man, how vain and foolish his thinking, how ignorant his conception of his office, how little reason we have to marvel at such a person were he to answer: On the strength of these external pastoral virtues and deeds—which later may be summed up in my obituary—I am a pastor, an evangelical minister of the Word of God! Now, it is just the really exemplary man who would back away from all these qualifications with a pained smile. He would have nothing to do with the fulfilment of a list of pastoral virtues and deeds. He would have nothing to do with something which would give him honor as a man and add to the glory of his necrology. He would most earnestly point us to another factor which does not belong to this series of pastoral virtues and deeds; a factor, however, which is in truth the foundation of his office and which makes his labor as a minister of the Word necessary, possible, and acceptable. We will have little understood our task today to do justice to the essence of the ministry of the Word of God if we would not now turn our whole attention to this other factor.

What is this other factor? It might be in keeping at this point to simply recall those words with which the Apostle Paul pointed to the foundation of his own office and that of his colleagues and their followers. "And I thank Christ Jesus our Lord, who has enabled me, for that he counted me faithful, putting me into the ministry; who was before a blasphemer, and a persecutor, and injurious! But I obtained mercy, because I did it ignorantly in unbelief! And the grace of our Lord was exceeding abundant with faith and love which is in Christ Jesus. This is a faithful saying, and worthy of all acceptation that Christ Jesus came into the world to save sinners; of whom I am chief. Howbeit, for this cause, I obtained mercy, that in me first Jesus Christ might show forth all longsuffering, for a pattern to them which should hereafter believe on him to life everlasting" (I Timothy 1: 12-16). "Who hath saved us, and called us with an holy calling, not according to our works, but according to his own purpose and grace, which was given in Christ Jesus before the world began, but is now made manifest by the appearing of our Savior Jesus Christ who hath abolished death, and hath brought life and immortality to light through the gospel" (II Timothy 1: 9-10).

We learn the following from these passages:

1. The ministry of the Word of God is primarily and decidedly a service of which we ourselves have need, and which the Word of God itself has shown and still shows us, and will continue to show unto us. It is not *our* service of which the Word of God has need, nor is it a service which we needed to, or could, render to the Word! It is not a patronizing service which we might render; nor an advertisement which we could make; nor an apology which

we, as a lawyer, would have to defend. And we are certainly not ministers of the Word if we feel ourselves called to be benevolent protectors, or big-hearted friends or representatives of whom the Word of God has need. "The word of God is not bound," (II Timothy 2: 9) —let whatever fate befall us.

"If we believe not (are not faithful), yet he abideth faithful: he cannot deny himself" (II Timothy 2: 13). "Nevertheless the foundation of God standeth sure" (II Timothy 2: 19). We do not need to make the foundation for the house of God, nor build it. "The Church of the living God, the pillar and ground of the truth" (I Timothy 3: 15). The "testimony of our Lord" (II Timothy 1: 8), which has founded and builded the Church is what we have to face, which needs not to be laid again and which needs no supplement. It was laid once and for all "before Pontius Pilate" (I Timothy 6: 13). It "appeared" (Titus 3: 4), finally appeared and was brought to light. In it we live. It is not ours, but God's, our Saviour's. It appeared "after the kindness and love of God our Saviour toward man" (Titus 3: 4). It appeared before we ever came to the remarkable idea of studying theology, before we were born, before all the encouraging and discouraging problems of our pastoral office and our life ever existed. Before all that, we heard, He had abolished death. Even before we asked what we could be, or do, for the Word of God, or before the question had any meaning, there stood, like a Gibraltar, the fact: He, the Lord, who is Himself the Word, Jesus Christ, "gave himself for us, that he might redeem us from all iniquity and purify unto himself a peculiar people" (Titus 2: 15; I Timothy 2: 6). He did this primarily and specifically for us ministers of the Word. Our inquiry as to what we can be or do for the Word of God can mean in every case only this: What can we be or do as those for whom Jesus Christ has already been and done everything? The answer to this question is our service to the Word of God.

Our ministry is based upon the fact that we have been shown mercy. Jesus Christ has exercised His great patience toward us. Our service rests in the fact that we are thankful with a thankfulness which does not think of any reward, nor pride itself on any merit of its own. Such service consists in that we have the most desperate need of Jesus Christ only as the one

to intercede for us in the eternal judgment of
God in which none of us can defend himself
nor be his own apologist. We feel that we are
absolutely redeemed, sustained, comforted,
justified, and made to rejoice through Him.
This necessity and freedom are ours, and they
alone make up specifically ministers of the
Word of God, to be an example for those who
should believe in Him unto life eternal! Jesus
Christ Himself makes us servants. He does
it solely through His caring to save sinners.
He does it because it is true that He came to
save sinners, and because we allow that truth
to be true!

2. The ministry to the Word of God is only
the peculiar, conscious, and specific activity
and task at that point—and there becomes self-
evident to all—where the Word of God is heard
(in faith). What Paul has to say regarding
his call to be an apostle does not fundamentally
overlook what has been said regarding the calling through and for Christ, or the calling of
the Church. "For the grace of God that
bringeth salvation hath appeared to all men"
(Titus 2: 11). "God will have all men to be
saved and come to the knowledge of the truth"
(I Timothy 2: 4). The apostle makes no

other claim for a genuine apostleship than this;
nor can his pupils, Timothy and Titus; nor
can we. We are, what we are, by virtue of
grace and long suffering, "the washing of re-
generation, and renewing of the Holy Ghost"
(Titus 3: 5). Upon the basis of this "knowing," to know "how thou oughtest to behave
thyself in the house of God" (I Timothy
3: 15). Upon this basis we will learn and expound the "godly edifying which is in faith"
(I Timothy 1: 4). What sort of an honorable
distinction is that? Paul knows only that of
all sinners he is chief! As such a sinner the
will of God (II Timothy 1: 1) made him to
be an apostle, and God gave him his task
(I Timothy 1: 1).

Is not this distinction a humiliation. Is it
not true that here the last shall be first? Is it
not true that here those upon whom God has
shown a peculiar mercy and patience have special need of them? Must we not be especially
distinguished in this respect in order to be ministers of the Word? Is not this humiliation
the secret of the fact that there must be bishops,
elders, preachers, teachers, servants in the
Church of Jesus Christ as well as other individuals, who, in an especial way have to be, and

do, that necessary thing in all Churches—and the Church is a house with many open doors and windows—namely, that which God desires and demands of all men?

But regardless as to what must be, the Churchly office of the ministry of the Word is an office of the whole Church as such. One cannot magnify *his* peculiar office in the Church with greater power than to understand it as a *general* office of the Church. It is a peculiar office only so far that in it the place of God's grace, as revelation and calling and God's election of man, becomes manifest. The Church is the assembly of those who have heard the Word, of those who are thankful and who do not think of any reward, nor feel they have any merit of their own. In such an assembly the service to the Word takes place out of the power of that one grace which is given the assembly, to call together the elect of God so "that they may also obtain the salvation which is in Christ Jesus" (II Timothy 2: 10), to remind this gathering that they, as a whole and as individual members, live by the power of this grace alone, but that they may and should really live by this grace (Titus 3: 8). And as we have not built, nor could have built, the house of God, so it does not belong to us, and it is not ours to lord it over the house of God. Now, if those in the assembly of the house of God are such people, from whom all power of enactment has been taken, and who have been justified through the grace of Jesus Christ (Titus 3: 7), how shall we justify the "steward" (Titus 1: 7) of the house of God his right to possess things, to be ruler of the members?

That person is a "steward" in the house of God, a minister of the Word, who, of all those in the house of God, has heard so urgently what has been said to them that he can say: We live in the midst of the living revelation of Christ, that revelation which has already occurred and that which shall yet occur (Titus 2: 11-14). We live between the Word which we have heard in all its sufficiency and that Word which we must hear in all its overpowering novelty. We do not live between birth and death; we live between baptism and the Lord's Supper. We do not live in the present; we live by that constant reminder of that which has been in an expectation of that which is to come. We do not live in our time; we live in God's time. We live in this brief, dark, and yet not totally dark world. It is brief and semi-dark because from its beginning and its end there streams the light of banished night from two brilliant Days of God, which in truth are not two Days, but the one Day of Jesus Christ, the Day that was and the Day which is coming. It is! In the midst of the night which is our day, that Day is! The only foundation of the Church consists in the fact that this night is encompassed by this Day of Jesus Christ and that this Day of Jesus Christ is our Day of life. *This makes us to be ministers of the Word!* Jesus Christ makes us his servants, and it is only through the truth that we are in the Church, whose Lord is Jesus Christ, that we are ministers of the Word, only because this is true and we allow it to be true, are we servants.

3. The ministry of the Word of God is a certain human living and acting, which is germinated and directed, ordered and achieved through Jesus Christ. We do not say it is a service because or through "God," nor do we call it a service performed because of the grace, mercy, and patience of God revealed through Jesus Christ—although that, of course, might be true. But, in speaking in this general way about "God," certain *human* ideas might be

a projection which we may form and decide, or arrange and manage.

Now this is something that cannot be taken into consideration at all in the service of the Word. Paul warned his disciples against nothing so urgently as against "myths" (I Timothy 1: 4; 4: 7; II Timothy 4: 4), against "oppositions of science" (gnosis), so-called (I Timothy 6: 20), against "seducing spirits," and the "doctrines of devils" (demons) (I Timothy 4: 1), against unwatchfulness (II Timothy 4: 5), against self-willed egotism (Titus 1: 7), against insubordination (Titus 1: 10), against prejudice and against partiality (I Timothy 5: 21). I take it that the well-known word about "youthful lusts" which Timothy should "flee" (II Timothy 2: 22) is, according to the context, not a reference to the particular sexual and similar human urge but in this connection refers, in a deeper and more comprehensive sense, to that primal urge of man to be his own master, leader, and creator. This urge can lead only to a place where man "becomes perverse and of a corrupt mind, and destitute of the truth," so that his reasoning capacity deteriorates and he is bereft of the truth (I Timothy 6: 5; II Timothy 2: 18; 4: 4). Being himself full of erroneousness, he leads others into error (II Timothy 3: 13).

On the contrary, Timothy should "follow righteousness, faith, charity, peace, with them that call on the Lord out of a pure heart" (II Timothy 2: 22). The inner content of these ideas is not to be found arbitrarily, according to Pauline words. On the contrary, the true inner content is in Jesus Christ, in the concrete form of his manifestation as true God and true man. So, "follow after righteousness" does not mean to chase after certain ideas and ideals. Rather, it means keep in remembrance "that Jesus Christ of the seed of David was raised from the dead!" (II Timothy 2: 8). This means to "exercise yourself in godliness" (I Timothy 4: 7).

"Godliness" is to turn one's gaze and attention to that mystery of incarnation, the humiliation (kenosis) of God, revealed in the resurrection of Christ (I Timothy 3: 16). What makes the servant of the Word is that he holds "the mystery of the faith in a pure conscience" (I Timothy 3: 9). He stands or falls with the purity of his conscience in this matter, with his confidential knowledge of this mystery. He must "chase after" it, because in it, and it alone, does he possess his unique existence, and in it he is either pardoned or condemned. Only in it is it true that Christ died and arose from the dead. "If we suffer with him, we shall also live with him." He is pardoned or condemned, according as he allows this truth to be true! "If we suffer, we shall also reign with him; if we deny him, he also will deny us" (II Timothy 2: 12). "For therefore we both labor and suffer reproach (struggle), because we trust in the living God" (I Timothy 4: 10). Of what value is anything else, if we are deprived of this hope? Of what avail all our own labor and struggle, which does not issue from this origin and end of our short night of life in which we pilgrim? And even though it were the mightiest labor in the love of God and neighbor, it might have the *form* but not the *power* of "godliness" (II Timothy 3: 5). Such a labor, or task, might be a waste of time in the light of true service to the Word, in spite of which we would still be indebted to God and man for something that rightfully belonged to them.

There are no other points of view or objectives which can agree with this hope on the living God. That we have this hope makes us servants of the Word. We must repeat: Jesus Christ Himself makes us His servants, and, indeed, because He became true man and true God, *Immanuel, God with us.*

This is that "other" factor which makes one a minister of the Word, in contrast with all other ever-so-respectable examples of mankind. So, to sum it all up, we could say: Jesus Christ as the Savior of sinners, as Lord of the Church, as eternal Son of God in the midst of our temporal existence—He it is who calls, and it is His call which makes men to be His servants. No one and nothing else! He makes actual people to be His servants, He makes human life and action to be His service. How else could He be Immanuel, "God with us"? There is Paul, there is Timothy, there is Titus; here are we, all of us, in our more-or-less cultured humanity. And as the question regarding the nature of our service to the Word is one that is told to us, so it is with the answer. What does this call mean for our lives? What obligations are enjoined upon us, of what are we apprised? What is there that breaks in upon us from beyond the human realm? If we again turn to the letters of Timothy and Titus, we will be apprised of three things.

1. As those who are called by Jesus Christ, we have a specific task to fulfill. This task consists in telling others what we have heard, namely, that Jesus Christ is the Savior, the' Lord, the Word of God in the flesh. In that we say this, we serve the Word of God. God does not helplessly need this service, but He desires and expects it. But this simple thankfulness, this plain adherence to the Church, this dependent attentiveness upon the mystery of faith—even these demand linguistic expression, for they call the brothers and the sisters, they wait upon them and see them potential in every fellow-man. The way to them, which for Christ's sake is our obligation, is through speech with them. We would not be in the service of the Word if we denied them our word. We have not heard anything ourselves, if we have nothing to say to them. We have an immense lot to tell them, regardless as to whether we succeed, even badly succeed, or do not succeed at all, in telling them. This is what the Apostle repeatedly called the obligation of "teaching." He designated himself always primarily as a "herald, apostle (one sent), teacher" (I Timothy 2: 7; II Timothy 1: 11). "These things

command and teach" (I Timothy 4: 11; 6: 3).
"Preach the word; be instant in season, out
of season" (II Timothy 4: 2). "But speak
thou the things which become sound doctrine"
(Titus 2: 1). This note is sounded again and
again.

The word "teaching," or "doctrine," has
become a word with a hard and meaningless
sound, simply because we no longer understand it. By this word we usually understand
an exposition of some sort of pedagogical, arbitrarily devised and constructed ideas, truths
and convictions. We are right in dimly sur-
mising that this cannot be called ministry to
the Word of God. By "doctrine," the apostle
understands the absolute opposite. For him,
doctrine is slightly disciplined, because its subject rests totally upon, and is bound in reference to, the Lord of man, his Word, His will,
His dealings with man. "Doctrine," in the
understanding of the apostle, means that man
is a learner over against God, and certainly
man is not an arbitrary speculator. God dwells
"in a light no man can approach, whom no man
hath seen, nor can see" (I Timothy 6:16).
But He reveals Himself because of His grace
and still reveals Himself. "Doctrine" is, there-

fore, that service to the Word, because the
world must know about this grace, and because
the Church must always remember that grace
is grace! The world does not know it is lost
and redeemed. This it must be told, and this it
must hear. And the Church must never forget
that grace is a free act of God. This it must
be told, and this it must hear.

Of this we may be assured: This "doctrine"
must always be life and work! "Do the work
of an evangelist" (II Timothy 4:5). If we
did it, if it was done in the Church, we would
not need to fret about life and work to com-
plement the doctrine. But if we fret about this
"practical" expression, or completion, of the
doctrine, it is because our "doctrine" is no
longer, or not yet, the apostolic, the truly
"practical," doctrine! And no complementary
expression, be it ever so glorious or splendid,
can make the failure good.

The "work of an evangelist" does not consist in proclaiming "ideals." It does not consist in criticizing man, his failures, his weak-
nesses, or his arrogance. It does not consist
in the Kierkegaardian critique of the "religious
man." It does not consist in *commanding* men
to love God and each other, nor in preaching

a social hope. It does not consist in giving a description of the evolution of this or that point of dogmatics, even if it is the best dogmatics.

The "work of an evangelist"—while he may make use of every possible material—is in what his name indicates. It consists in proclaiming the Evangel. The proclamation of the gospel is the proclamation of Jesus Christ. If Jesus Christ is the content, if it is "grace, nothing but grace, and the whole of grace," then there is no need of a supporting practical effect of some deed, because it itself is, and does, the one true deed. The Church waits upon this deed, and the world awaits the action of this deed from the Church. We must learn again to do this work sincerely and thoroughly.

2. As those who are called by Jesus Christ, we have a definite burden to bear. Paul speaks again and again about the suffering which he and his disciples had to take upon themselves, especially in the second letter to Timothy. "I am ready to be offered up and the time of my departure is at hand" (II Timothy 4:6). And you, "endure hardness, as a good soldier of Jesus Christ" (II Timothy 2:3; 4:5). We cannot evade the fact that this suffering has no casual meaning for Paul. Rather, it is more

an unavoidable accompanying phenomenon of his service to the Word. Therefore, because I am a herald, an apostle, and a teacher, "for which cause I also suffer these things" (II Timothy 1: 8), or the gospel, "I suffer trouble, as an evil doer, even unto bonds" (II Timothy 1: 8). The meaning is evident. The gospel itself suffers, and not because the world, in which it is proclaimed, is evil. No, on the contrary, it suffers because the gospel is the power of God which is preached in an evil world. For that reason, the necessary suffering of a servant of the Word is no sad or fatally resigned suffering, but surely a joyous suffering. This suffering is the necessary outer border, the sign of a great reality: *Christus vivit Christus regnat, Christus triumphat!* For that reason, suffering is inevitable for faithful servants.

Note carefully that Paul and the New Testament in general do not speak of this suffering in any case as a "witness" which might be made into, or a part of, the proclamation of the gospel.

Witness is only that which takes place under "Pontius Pilate" (I Timothy 6: 13), not that which takes place in Antioch, Iconium, or

Lystra (II Timothy 3: 11), and which, is classed as suffering. This suffering is, however, very important, since "all that will live godly in Christ Jesus shall suffer persecution" (II Timothy 3: 12). Not that this suffering should be edifying to others or become for them a sentimentally heroic spectacle or example, but that the sufferers might give themselves the necessary comfort. Christ suffers, the gospel suffers, and when Christ suffers He triumphs. In the suffering of the gospel, it expresses its godly power. In this achievement the servants must and may be present without "shame" (II Timothy 1: 8). This means that they stand by without wishing it otherwise when the world, in which Christ is triumphantly proclaimed, reveals itself as an evil world.

It is the fate of every servant of the Word that he must endure the contradiction and the antagonism of the world which always seeks and holds to a god other than the One who reveals Himself through and as grace. He must also suffer the contradiction and the antagonism of the Church, which again and again does not care to grant that grace is grace! The world gladly grants that God *is* free, the Church will not grant that God *remains* free!

But he to whom it is given to proclaim the kingdom of God must say *that* to the world and the Church. Therefore, he will be contradicted and opposed. If he did not need to suffer that, he would be no preacher of grace. The priest of the gods, and the expositions of the law, do not, for this reason, need to suffer. We would need only to join them to be rid of our burden. As ministers of the Word, we will bear our burden, not with complaints against Church and world, but with hope for both, not in stoical indifference but in Christian joy. We will bear with joy the fate and the burden of being such men who are contradicted and opposed from all sides.

3. As those who are called of Jesus Christ, we have to enter into a definite life-situation. Our natural characters, our talents, and our experiences in life may be quite varied. One thing, however, is certain. Every minister of the Word is in a struggle day and night. A servant of Jesus Christ is, of necessity, "a good soldier" (II Timothy 2:3). It is a worthy struggle, which we are asked to engage in, one filled with promise, and the one really worthwhile struggle which may be engaged in on earth. But, because it is worthy, it is difficult,

the most difficult on earth. All worth-while and difficult struggles on earth come to a climax in this one! It is called "the good fight of faith." (I Timothy 6: 12). Faith itself is a combatant in this matter, and faith means our calling for and by Jesus Christ, through whom we are servants and ministers of the Word.

This calling of ours is threatened, is attacked, and must defend itself as long as there is a night between the two Days of Jesus Christ. It is never halted, but it is always threatened; never uncertain but always in danger; it is always maintained in new crises of decision! When we think of the task and burden of the minister of the Word, how can we be otherwise? How can we remain unattacked in the fulfilment of our task as a teacher? How can our "doctrine" be or remain "sound"? (I Timothy 1: 10; II Timothy 1: 13; Titus 1: 9; etc.).

Are we not placed in the midst of a veritable cosmos, or world, of human spirits, of others as well as our own, and are we not threatened with a maze of possibilities to "teach otherwise" (I Timothy 1: 3; 6: 3), which means to teach something other than the sovereignty of Christ, something other than "grace, only grace, and the whole of grace"? There is so much, yes beautiful, true, and good. But we remind ourselves that all else are "myths." Everything else means emptying and denaturing our "doctrine" (I Timothy 1:7; 6:10; II Timothy 2:16; Titus 1:10); it means an entrance into a battle of mere words which leads to nothing but catastrophe for the hearers (II Timothy 2:14); it indicates that we have been led astray, and are leading others away, from the faith (I Timothy 6:21; II Timothy 2:18). Faith alone can keep this from happening. But to that end faith must assert itself, watch itself, and suffer ever anew. Therefore, the fight of faith must be fought!

And how shall we avoid being attacked in bearing our burdens as sufferers? It is so much easier to be ashamed of the gospel in the face of this contradiction and antagonism which is in the world and in the Church. It is so much easier to become "entangled in the affairs of this life," with which affairs the minister of the Word must, of course, concern himself (II Timothy 2:4). It is easier to give these things first place in life. It is so much easier to suppose that "gain is godliness," easier to "make a business out of godliness" (I Timothy 6:5). It is so much easier to flee from the greater, apostolic pain, to the somewhat uncomfortable, but not so terrible pain of Mr. Everybody. To the end that this may not happen, the fight of faith must be fought.

Who dares to say with the apostle, "I have fought the good fight, I have run my course, I have kept the faith"? (II Timothy 4:7). These words on the lips of the apostle, as he stood on the threshold of death, are the words of a fighter. "And if a man also strive for mastery, yet is he not crowned except he strive lawfully" (II Timothy 2:5). Let us add to the word "lawfully" this phrase—the fight of faith is one set in the midst of the world and the Church. It is people who antagonize the servant of the Word as purveyors of error, contradiction, and opposition. Certainly, these people, whose word eats as a "cancer" (II Timothy 2:17) must be "refuted" for the sake of the bearers and the gospel (Titus 1:9), "whose mouths must be stopped" (Titus 1:11).

But even if this is a part of the fight of faith, it is not a fight *against,* but *for,* these people. The ministry of the Word can in no wise be understood as a fight of one party against a counter party. "I exhort that first of all"— thus it reads in reference to those people outside

in the world—"supplications, prayers, inter-
cessions, and giving of thanks be made for *all*
men . . . for this is good and acceptable in the
sight of God our Saviour; who will have all
men to be saved and come unto the knowledge
of the truth" (I Timothy 2: 1-4).

And in reference to the people of the world
who are more difficult to handle we read, "And
the servant of the Lord must not strive; but be
gentle unto all men, apt to teach, patient, in
meekness instructing those that oppose themselves; if God peradventure will give them repentance to the acknowledging of the truth"
(II Timothy 2: 24-25). Even the farthest
reaches of this statement do not mean a cross-
ing over into open warfare. "A man that is an
heretic after the first and second admonition reject; knowing that he that is such is subverted,
and sinneth, being condemned of himself"
(Titus 3: 10-11). If we think otherwise, if we
desire to carry on a party-strife for the gospel's
sake, then we are indeed fleeing from the true
fight of faith! The battle of faith is that struggle in which God maintains *His* right over
against us! How could God do anything else
for us? How could our calling to this fight

of faith be anything but one in which God holds Jacob fast and holds him under?

We will not be able to abolish this life-situation as ministers of the Word.

This is what the call through and for Jesus Christ means in the life of a person. It is a task, a burden, a situation. It is a doctrine, a suffering, a fight.

There still remains, in closing, a small, apparently insignificant, but highly fundamental, principle to consider. I want to say something in addition about the reason why I have based my theme so squarely and closely upon the Pauline pastoral letters. This close relation to these letters might have been less equivocal and confined, although it would not dare to have been omitted. In no case would we have been able to speak about this ministry of the Word of God without reference to these pastoral letters and to the Old and New Testaments. And this reference would not be silent or inexplicit, but in every case it would be a very specific attention to these letters and the Bible. For the ministry of the Word of God reminds us of its origin in the incarnation of the Word, also in this, that it is consummated in a visible human order. I would like to direct your attention to this order, because I have related myself so closely to the letters referred to above, in what has already been said.

Just as the sovereignty of Jesus Christ expresses itself among us in that there are parents, who exist of necessity, and whom children are to respect; just as there are masters whom servants obey; just as the husband is the head of the wife and not the reverse (in spite of all the things we may say about this order!), just so it is in regard to the ministry of the Word of God as a concrete form of grace. In this ministry, there is a definite and visible human overseership and subordination which is valid, and cannot be reversed. Paul speaks to Timothy as "a child" (I Timothy 1:1, 18; II Timothy 1:4). He challenged him to be as little ashamed of his apostleship as of the testimony of the Lord Himself (II Timothy 1:8). When Paul urges him to "stir up the gift that is in him" as one fans embers into a bright flame (I Timothy 4:14; II Timothy 1:6-7), he did not fail to remind Timothy of the "laying on of hands" through which he received this gift, which, while it was not thus mediated, nevertheless accompanied it. Everything hinges on whether he "continues" with what he "has learned and has been assured of" (I Timothy 4: 16; II Timothy 3: 14). A minister of the Word is "nourished up in the words of faith and good doctrine," which have not begun with him as a human reality, but which he has "followed after" (I Timothy 4: 6; II Timothy 3: 10).

He has been entrusted with a prophecy which went before him (I Timothy 1: 18), which he should guard (I Timothy 6: 20; II Timothy 1: 12, 14), for he must pass it on to others (II Timothy 2: 2). He has been given a command which he must keep before him unaltered and unrebuked, "without spot, unrebukable, until the appearing of our Lord Jesus Christ" (I Timothy 6: 14). From a child he has "known the Holy Scriptures, which are able to make you wise unto salvation through faith which is in Jesus Christ" (II Timothy 3: 15).

Therefore, there can be no lasting doctrine without "attendance to reading" (I Timothy 4: 13). For the Scriptures, and indeed the whole of the Scriptures, is the "bearer of the breath of God," and, therefore, it is such as to be "profitable for doctrine, for reproof, for correction, for instruction in righteousness;

that the man of God may be perfect, thoroughly furnished unto all good works" (II Timothy 3:16). Perhaps we are confronting in this passage the place where the mystery of the ministry of the Word of God (which has stirred our thought today) is easy to grasp and see for everyone, if not in its central core and essence. A minister of the Word is a concretely bound man; bound to the Word which has become flesh and who is, therefore, bound to the witness of his prophets and apostles.

We have touched very slightly upon one central, important biblical concept, because it is, remarkably, so slightly touched upon in the pastoral letters which we have followed so closely. It is the concept of the Holy Spirit. It is, perhaps, necessary to bring the Holy Spirit into consideration because, in the mind of the Apostle, the work of the Holy Spirit in respect to the ministry of the Word is self-evidently this "following after," "remaining in," "watching over," and "holding to," that which they have received from the prophets and the apostles.

The work of the Holy Spirit is the concrete relationship to prophets and apostles in which they find themselves. Perhaps we ought to ask ourselves uneasily about the work of the Holy Spirit in our office, and through our office in the Church, and through the Church in the world, simply because this concrete relationship has become alien to us, as has the blessedness, the freedom, the joy of our service which can be achieved only in this relationship. Perhaps, in our sincere zeal to serve God and only God, in our zeal to serve the Christian order—which is not reversible as between overseership and subordination; perhaps the discipline demanded of service to the Word, in which God can be served as He wills and demands to be served has become strange and foreign to us, in that *we really serve ourselves* in our holy ardor.

I have said this because I wanted to give an answer to the question I raised about the work of the Holy Spirit. This is certain, we could not even put this question if we did not, in all of our ministry of the Word, keep before us this ultimate, extremely conservative and yet extremely radical principle, which Calvin delighted to express: We must become pupils of the Holy Scriptures!

THE CHRISTIAN AS A WITNESS

I SHALL try to answer the question which our theme implies by speaking of what may be learned from the Holy Scriptures, according to my understanding and judgment, concerning the concepts of witness and testimony. I have formulated my insights in six theses. It is my task to amplify them by a brief explanation of each.

I. *Testimony is a word of man which has been given of God, the capacity of reminding other men of God's reign, grace, and judgment. Where a human word (speech) has this capacity, there is Church.*

1. *Testimony is a word of man.* Whenever the Holy Scriptures makes use of the terms "testimony" and "witnesses," they always signify human speech addressed by a man to other men. It means words such as men are able to speak and hear. This is also the understanding of the Holy Scriptures when it says that God Himself bears testimony, or that angels

are His messengers, or when, as in the Old
Testament, the tables of the law and other ob-
jects are called testimonies of God. It is always speech addressed to men. And when we
are told in Romans 2: 15 that "the conscience
bears witness," we are told also that "the work
of the law" is written in their hearts. It is legi-
ble there; it is intelligent speech.

There are other manifestations of God.
God communicates with men also by deeds.
The Bible calls such manifestations "signs."
But, as a whole, when it speaks of testimony, it
means a word spoken by a man to other men.
Exceptions, such as John 5:36, or Hebrews
2: 4, where works are designated a testimony,
only serve to confirm the rule.

2. It is *the task* of this human word *to remind other men of God's reign, grace, and
judgment.* The term "witness" is borrowed
from the language of the judiciary and of law.
It conveys the thought that God makes use of
witnesses because a law suit is in progress between God and man. God's cause is at stake;
God's right must be vindicated. In this law
suit God calls witnesses against men who have
apostatized and who are hardened against
Him and meet Him with hostile intent. The

witnesses whom He calls bear witness of His
reign, grace, and judgment.   In the Old Testament, they testify of the covenant which God
has made with His people.   In the New Testament, they testify of the deeds, the suffering,
death, and resurrection of Jesus Christ, of the
revelation of the mystery of God which has
been made manifest in Him.   "And ye are witnesses of these things" (Luke 24:48), or (John
1:2)—"we have seen it, and bear witness, and
show unto you that eternal life," and (1 John
5:11)—"this is the record, that God hath given
to us eternal life, and this life is in his Son."

3.   Testimony is human word *which has
been given the capacity of God.*   Testimony, in
the meaning of the Holy Scriptures, is a word
which possesses a definite and specific dynamic.
It is not self-evident that there are such words
and such a speech carrying within them the obligation to remind other men of God's reign,
grace, and judgment.   As little as it is natural
that there are such things as God's reign,
grace, and judgment, so little is it natural that
we have testimony of it, *i.e.,* witnesses who are
called and enabled to this function, and who
have the authority and power to bear such witness.   Not every man is a witness.   The proph-

ets, apostles, and disciples are such witnesses (Neh. 9: 30). According to the Holy Scriptures, the power of their testimony does not rest in a special quality of their own, neither in their piety, nor in their deeds, and not even in their suffering as the later concept of "martyr" has it; it rests wholly and exclusively in that God, in his law suit against men, chooses these men in particular, and makes disciples, apostles, and prophets to serve Him as His witnesses in His cause.

4. *Where human word has this capacity, there is a Church.* Church, in the meaning of the Holy Scriptures, is the place where this law suit between God and man is conducted and in the course of which God calls such men to be His witnesses. In the Old Testament, the people of Israel form the Church; in the New Testament, it is the ecclesia, the Church of Jesus Christ, "Upon this rock (Matthew 16: 18) I will build my church." Or as in Ephesians 2: 20, "So then ye are built upon the foundation of the apostles and prophets, Jesus Christ himself being the chief cornerstone." Where *this* dynamic word of *the* testimony is spoken and heard, there is "the Church."

II. *The original and real witness of God is*

*not man but God Himself. By His command,
and in His service, men become, are, and remain, witnesses of His own testimony.*

With this thesis, we are entering the very
heart of our deliberations. This thesis is altogether decisive. If I am able to tell you here
what needs to be said, I shall have it said rightly; and if you understand here what needs to
be understood, you will have rightly understood.

We must recall here the reference we made
to Ephesians 2: 20 about "Jesus Christ himself being the chief cornerstone." Comparison ought to be made with 1 John 5: 9, "If we
receive the witness of men, the witness of God
is greater . . . ." It will surely not surprise us
now, if we are compelled to state that the Holy
Scriptures do not make mention of this man
or that man as the one who bears real testimony of God unmistakably, it is God Himself,
although our definition about testimony as
human word remains valid.

We could quote a long list of passages, from
the New Testament no less than from the Old.
It is God who bears testimony of God:—the
Father, as says the Gospel of John; or Jesus
Christ as in Revelation 1: 5, or the Holy Spirit

as in 1 John 5: 7, "It is the Spirit that beareth witness, because the Spirit is the truth."

According to the Holy Scriptures, truth is God's self-revealing and self-communicating reality. How is it possible otherwise? Can we conceive of man being capable to be God's witness? Only God Himself can be God's witness according to all that the Holy Scriptures predicate of God and man. Man is a creature, mortal, a sinner, and an apostate. How shall such a man qualify as a witness of God? God Himself must speak for God, and God alone is adequate as God's witness. This insight may well be called fundamental and necessary in any man who, on his part, becomes a witness of God. In fact, every real witness has known and confessed: God is His own witness. God cannot use *my* testimony. I am not an apt instrument in His hands. If God makes use of men, nevertheless, a miracle is happening. If I speak, I speak because God Himself speaks, and my speaking can therefore become always and only reference to God's own Word.

The original and real witness is God Himself and He alone. But God lets the miracle happen, lets it happen in the mystery of His

will, that there are, nevertheless, men who are
witnesses of Him.   Neither are we able to solve
this mystery, nor do we have a rationale for it,
nor shall we ever be able to prove its reality.
But He commands and it is done.   He wills to
have it so, and so it is.   For God's sake there
are prophets, apostles, and disciples.   This
majestic God, dwelling in His own mystery
and in a light which no man can approach, *He*
calls.   *He* sends, *He* lays words on the lips of
men which they are to speak in His name.   We
can only understand a passage like Acts 1:18
"Ye shall be my witnesses" as a record of an
incomprehensible condescension on the part of
God.   This God, so holy and so merciful, this
God who is so far removed from us, draws so
near to us that there are men of whom it is true:
"Ye shall be my witnesses."

The record of John the Baptist (John 1, 6:
19) is a comprehensive portrayal of what the
Bible understands by a witness.   After mention has been made of the unspeakable mystery
of God, it is further said, "There was a man
sent from God, whose name was John.   He
was not that light, but was sent to bear witness
of that light."   It is God's grace that there are
men who are sent from God.   But even so, it is

the grace of *God,* and it means: *he,* John, was *not* that "Light." God bears witness, and man assists. Recognition of this truth is a fundamental condition of every real witness who is a genuine witness of God, namely, that he recognizes this truth. With it the possibility of men being witnesses stands or falls. God is His own witness, and by an incomprehensible miracle of His mercy I am placed in the position of being permitted to be a witness of His own testimony. This insight and confession constitutes the dignity of the man who is a witness, and it must be the axiom of his testimony.

The three theses which follow, III, IV, and V, belong together. In them I shall attempt to answer what you may call "practical questions." How does a man *become* God's witness? How *is* a man God's witness? How does a man *remain* God's witness? The decisive and comprehensive answer to these three questions has been given in the second thesis. We now presuppose its validity for the following theses. A man becomes, is, and remains, God's witness because God Himself bears testimony concerning Himself. Where He does give it, and only there, a man becomes a servant of God's own testimony. Permit me to explain more in detail this general and comprehensive answer.

III. *A man becomes God's witness in gratitude that God has already granted us His own testimony.*

The first of the three questions asks: How does a man become a witness? What needs to be said in answer to this question I have summed up, in the language of the Holy Scriptures, in the word gratitude, or thankfulness? A man becomes a witness in his acknowledgment that God's own testimony is granted us because God has freely given it to us. Gratitude is antithetical to every arbitrary venture. Gratitude prohibits every undertaking in which a man ascribes to himself aptitude and capacity to be God's witness. A real witness knows that he has been *made* a witness, and that he is *called* to be a witness. He knows that God's testimony has already been given to him and to the world. The thankfulness of a genuine witness, the gratitude in which he becomes a witness, may consist, however, not only in this that he knows: God is in heaven, and we are on earth; God is Lord and we are His servants.

According to the Holy Scriptures this gratitude must be a concrete gratitude in which a man does not only have his eyes fixed on heaven, but in which he finds God's testimony on the earth also, in his life and in the actuality of human history. A real witness of God does not begin with the notion that he is the first witness. He looks back on witnesses who have gone before. He accepts their testimony as God's testimony to him. He is obedient to God *and* is attentive to these men who have given him this testimony. Think of Psalm 119. In 176 verses we hear one truth repeated: Of this we live, in this we hope, on this we look, this we will hear and say: God's witness! God's right! God's statutes! In saying this, the writer of this psalm becomes truly a witness himself. He acknowledges that testimony exists already. It is the attitude of the whole of the Scriptures. The prophets do not begin with some kind of an enthusiasm. Rather, they take their stand on the foundation of the covenant which God has previously made with Israel, and they repeat only what Jehovah has of old said to his people. They join their progenitors and they proclaim God's ways, in reverent retrospect and respect. We do not find a different attitude in the New Testament. Jesus says, "I came not to destroy the law" (Matthew 5: 17), and we need to understand this word quite concretely. In a similar manner, Paul, who felt perhaps more keenly than the other apostles the new thing that has entered the world in Jesus Christ, can and must say, "A righteousness of God hath been manifested, being witnessed by the law and the prophets" (Romans 3: 21). As a herald of Jesus Christ, he takes his place in the ranks of the witnesses who have preceded him in the old covenant. The wholly new message which he has to bring, he repeats as one which is not new at all; for God has borne testimony of Himself from of old.

In sum, if we as Christians would become witnesses, the primary question for us to ask is not, Do I have the Holy Spirit? What do I do in the Holy Spirit? Everything depends, however, on a very clear apprehension on our part of what it means that we have been baptized and, therefore, belong to the Church of Jesus Christ and to the Church of God. In the remembrance of our baptism, we have also a memorial of the certitude of the word which overcomes the world, because in our baptism we are reminded of the word which has already overcome us. The large question which every true witness must face in the beginning of his way is just this: Have you been told something before you go and say something to others?

In the course of the discussion, the question arose if what Christians are told applies with equal force to the world also? It seems to me the question has failed to give due consideration to what has been suggested concerning gratitude. If the life of a witness of Jesus Christ has its realistic beginning in gratitude for the testimony which God has given him, then it is impossible to think of saying to the world anything but this one thing. It will be the chief and only concern of such a man to repeat the one message of which prophets and apostles have borne witness. The question which confronts us as we enter the office of a witness will be: Are you thankful enough for what you yourself have received? And in gratitude for this already existing testimony gratitude will mirror God's own testimony to us whose servants we now desire to be. If we cannot be grateful, we shall hardly understand the basic condition of God's own testimony

which alone is able to make a man His witness
by the miracle of His mercy.

IV. *A man is God's witness in reverence as
he subordinates his own word to the testimony
of God Himself.*

The second question we asked was this:
How does it happen that a man really does
bear witness of God? I have summed up the
answer to this question in the word *reverence.*
Reverence is the attitude of a servant toward
his master. It is the attitude of a man who
may not carry out a plan of his own but must
await a command. I would like to remind
you of the closely related word "respect." The
word "respect" is derived from respicere, which
means to look to. Where a man looks to what
God has commanded, he bears testimony.

We stand once again before the fact that a
witness is a man whose autonomy has been attacked. He can no longer be his own master;
he is constrained to obey. Let me remind you
again of John the Baptist. John 5: 35 says of
him, "He was the lamp that shineth and burn-
eth." And in another place he is called "a man
sent from God." This John, however, does not
have a message of his own making to communi-
cate, nor a truth of whose validity and impor-

tance he has persuaded himself. His message
is the message of another. John 3: 29 says,
"He that hath the bride is the bridegroom."
John points to Jesus Christ. Again he says,
"Behold, the Lamb of God!" (John 1: 36).
John the Baptist, for the very reason that he
is a genuine witness, only makes reference to
another. He has no subsistence of his own.
He is without importance of his own. He only
functions as he bears witness of another and
points away from himself to another. This is
what makes him truly great. "He must increase, but I must decrease" (John 3: 30). In
him we are able to see that a witness is not a
man who presents a theme of his own, or who
has a subject which moves him deeply and fills
his life. A witness does not come with the
claim, *I* have something to say. Surely, he has
something to say. But what he says can only
be a reminder of what God has said and wants
to have said. He functions in strict subordination.

This brings us to an important axiom of all
Christian testimony. The Church is not in the
world to present a message about certain ideas
and directions concerning the condition of the
world. At bottom, the Church is in the world

only with a book in its hands. We have no other possibility to bear witness except to explain this book. And if we are asked, What have you to say?, we can only answer, Here something has been said and what is said we want to hear. Whenever we make our own ideas our theme and subject, our testimony is no longer pure. The speaker is then no longer like unto John who says, He must increase and I must decrease. He may be a little bit of a philosopher, perhaps a bit of a theologian. He may be very much moved, very passionate, very sincere, and very well-meaning. But he is no longer what the Scriptures call a witness. In the meaning of the Holy Scriptures, a witness is a man who expounds, explains, interprets; a man who points to the place where prophets and apostles have spoken.

Certainly, even the witness will have ideas and convictions of his own. He occupies a place in human life; he lives in the midst of definite historical situations. But in and beyond these incidental factors of his existence, everything depends on whether he subordinates himself as he says the words, He is the Lord, and I am His servant. Whatever testimony is spoken in a realization of this subordination will be genuine testimony. We shall not be able to prevent giving voice to our ideas and convictions also; but we must be on guard against being a second master besides Him who alone is Primary Lord. Subordination means this very concrete discipline. It is not merely subordination under God in heaven. Our reverence must become concrete here on earth. Here on earth the book comes in and indicates to us the rule by which we must run our course. It was the rule of the prophets and apostles; and if Christians intend to be witnesses, they may not look for a rule which differs from theirs.

V. *A man remains a witness of God in the hope that God shall give us again His own testimony.*

As a third question we asked: How does a man *remain* a witness? In the Holy Scriptures, we hear of men who are and remain witnesses. We are informed that testimony is not only given here and there as lightning flashes from the heavens. Genuine testimony is always such a flash, to be sure. We hear, however, of the existence of witnesses whose life-task and life-calling it is to be witnesses. This fact forces us to ask, How is it possible for a man to remain a witness so that one is justified in expecting from him genuine testimony? How is it possible for this man to enter, and remain in, the ranks of which the apostles and prophets form the beginning. What makes him capable of representing the Church? What justifies our expectation that he will truly represent it, and thus be a reminder of God's reign, grace, and judgment?

We shall not escape saying here also: It is possible only in the miracle of God's mercy. God is not bound to any man, not even to His apostles and prophets. They are bound to Him. Prophets and apostles are what they are, not because of their personal qualities, not even on account of their religious and moral virtues. These qualities and virtues, although they surely have them, do not furnish a guarantee that they shall remain witnesses, for they function by the divine miracle only. If these men were witnesses not only now and then, but remained and continued to become witnesses, it was—and here we reach the concept of hope —because they reached out, and were fitted to this hope and expectation: The same God who has borne testimony of Himself and whom I may serve, will again bear witness of Himself.

If I am unfaithful, and I am unfaithful—in fact, a genuine witness knows and confesses it —God is and remains faithful. He does not withdraw His promise but will continue to fulfill it. A witness of God remains a witness in the truth by taking continual refuge in the petition: Come, Creator Spirit!   Creator! Christian life is not subject to, nor does it foster, the presumptive knowledge that the fountains before which we sit and whence we see the waters flow will just continue to flow. ⌐No, if they keep on flowing, if I continue to live a Christian life, it is because of God's creative activity.

In the first question, How does a man become a witness? I pointed to the sacrament of baptism.   In the present question, How does a man remain a witness? I refer you to the other Christian sacrament, the Lord's Supper. It proclaims, and is intended to proclaim, one truth only, namely, Christ makes complete intercession for us.   He feeds and nourishes us with His body and blood to everlasting life. *He!* The Lord's Supper is the sacrament of hope, of advent. We do not live our Christian life between birth and death, but between the two sacraments of baptism and the Lord's

Supper.   And in the midst of our life, the sacrament of the Lord's Supper proclaims, and continues to proclaim, the presence of Jesus Christ in our behalf.   It vouches for the presence of Jesus Christ as one who makes good where we fail.   Hope means to behold Jesus Christ as the One who makes restitution where and what we have defaulted.   A witness is always a man who is on his way to the Lord's Supper.   His eyes are ever on the advent of Christ in a firm hope: Christ for me!   And in that spirit he will remain a witness.   For he does not stand on the foundation of his own goodness and piety and sincerity but on the sole foundation that God will vindicate himself as God; for he has already justified himself in Jesus Christ *against* every man *for* every man. Since it has happened once for all—It is finished!—our future and the future of the world is clear, and the path through the world lies open also for the witness of Jesus Christ.   His stand is fixed under the sign: Thy kingdom come!

VI. *The Christian is, as witness, a man who flees from the wisdom and folly of his human word to the testimony of God.   The Church can*

*always be seen (visible) in this flight and never
and nowhere else.*

We come to the close of our deliberations.
The sixth thesis is a recapitulation. I intend
to repeat in somewhat different words what
has already been said. The Christian as a
witness is a disciple of the biblical witnesses.
If you have understood and grasped this, you
have understood what I meant to say. In this
connection I ought to tell you that it is much
easier to be a master than a student. Every
one of us prefers to be a master. It is everyone's desire to master the Bible and its witnesses. We would like to know what to do
with them. As genuine witnesses we can only
become, be, and remain students here. We
are in a school from which we shall not some
day be graduated in order to become masters
ourselves. On the contrary, the school in which
we are enrolled will make us increasingly students, and "free balloon sailings" are increasingly denied us.

What is it that we shall learn in the school of
these biblical witnesses? I have indicated it in
my thesis with the metaphor of flight. A flight
signifies, at all events, a very lively movement.

Provision is made, at any rate, that something is happening, and I live in hope that in the discussion which is to follow none of you will start the dreary song that activity is wanting. Flight signifies an extremely lively activity. It is a movement, a very lively movement indeed. And it has this advantage over many another movement that it is a very definite movement. A man in flight flees *from* something *to* something else. He has a Whence and a Whither. I have said in my thesis: Man flees from the wisdom and the folly of his human word. In great haste he must turn from one and from the other to the testimony of the biblical Word. Had I told you that he must turn from the *folly* of his human word, I would be assured of your understanding and agreement with me.

And indeed, he must turn from his folly also; he must not be foolish and mean. But the enemy from which a witness must flee appears on the horizon in his most realistic and dangerous form only if we understand that we must flee also, in fact very particularly, from the wisdom of our own word. Only when we see them both together, our dullness and our perspicacity, our insights and our errors, only then do we really understand what is happening. We shall become aware of the great obstacle which prevents our being God's witnesses. For is it not true that this mixture of wisdom and folly is none else than the man against whom God is conducting His law suit? Against him He has gone into action. It is this creature which God loves and wants to redeem. And in order that it may be done, God's testimony must be told him. If we are called upon to be God's witnesses, it is evident that we are dealing with two principals who are totally different from each other. On the one side, there is this wise *and* foolish creature, and on the other, God's testimony. And the path leads away from the one in the direction of the other. The twain will meet, to be sure. But they will truly meet only as the result of a movement from here to there. And it implies a confession on our part that God is right and I am wrong; God loves me and I live from the fact that He loves me.

The relation between these two principals may be compared with a dialogue in which one party does the speaking and the other the listening. Everything depends on a clear appreciation of the fact that we are taking flight away from ourselves to God's own testimony. We are compelled to flee, also and particularly, from our wisdom. For our wisdom is also a part of the man who stands in need of God. And now permit me to lay special emphasis on one particular aspect of our wisdom. For when I said "wisdom" I did not merely have in mind what we call "secular" or "profane" wisdom; definitely and emphatically I include our "Christian" wisdom, *e.g.,* the wisdom of our theology. A story was told here of a Japanese professor who found wisdom's final conclusion in this that he cherishes Karl Barth for his inner man and Karl Marx for the external. He is a classic example of a man who instead of fleeing from every wisdom seeks shelter there. What this Japanese should do above all is to take flight from the two "Karls," turn right about face, and hasten away with the greatest possible speed from here to there.

Are we in the condition in which we *know* that we must take to flight? Or do we still expect some good from our "Here"? In the proportion in which we do we disqualify ourselves for the office of God's witnesses. My Here is *my* starting point, but *starting* point only! Paul says, "I forget the things which are be-

hind, and stretch forward to the things which
are before" (Philippians 3: 13). On the other
side stands God's testimony. God is concretely and actually present in a word which is
spoken by man. We do not only possess a
word of our own wisdom and folly; no, there
exists also a Word of God's wisdom and folly.
We may be servants of this divine Word and
have our hope in it. Do we have it? Do we
know it? Most assuredly we do not flee from
here to there merely for the purpose of denying and condemning the world. No, the man
who has gained an understanding here turns
about and faces it in self-evident gladness because he knows a place to which he may flee,
a place which is ever waiting for him, namely,
God's testimony.

Two questions confront every one of us:
First, Has our wisdom and folly become something for us from which we must flee? Second,
Has God's wisdom and folly become to us the
strong fortress where we may take our refuge?
I cannot answer for every one of us. I can
only tell you that these are the critical points.
The answer to these questions decides whether
we are God's witnesses. I can only point you
to the prophets and apostles. They have made

the decision: From here to there! And if we are their disciples we shall do what genuine students do—we shall learn. If you had an ear for what I meant to say, you must have heard it is an admonition to enroll in the school in which this flight is taught. At all times and in all places the Church is seen on this flight, and never anywhere else. Wherever this school is in session we have a Church, and there the Headmaster is alone Master, and its students devote themselves alone to *His* instruction.

APPENDIX

A Discussion of the Address on The Christian as Witness

A LADY from America asks how the process which was called "flight" may be described in terms of psychology.

Karl Barth answers:—In answering this question, let me begin with saying that in my address I did not pretend to give a description of myself, but of a biblical witness. He is human, and therefore it must undoubtedly be possible to paraphrase his attitude with psychological categories also. It is impossible, however, to offer a general answer and description of what happens in the process which I have called a flight. The Oxford Movement was cited as an example. It urges its members to take down notes of their inward and external life. I would not exclude this possibility. But if some one were to come and tell me: A witness *must* take down notes, I would most

certainly say: No, a witness may be quite neg-
ligent in this respect. He may live his life without taking down a single note. But, on the other
hand, if some one were to say: You may not
take down notes, I should answer: I insist on
taking down notes! You understand, the psychological sphere in which witnesses live their
life is as broad as human life itself. The sign
of the flight is never unequivocal. A witness
may be very timid. He may be fleeing from
life outwardly also. On the other hand, a witness may be a very happy and stouthearted individual, who goes his way courageously, and
still be a fugitive in the meaning of my address.
It is quite impossible to give a fixed definition
of this process in the categories of psychology.

*   *   *

The next question (by an Englishman)
claims that the address tears God apart into a
Creator God and a Redeemer God. The
charge is made that the first is in truth not a
good God; for He has created man as an evil
creature since we are compelled to flee from
him. It urges further, that, in the law suit between God and man, man ought to be appreci-
ated not merely as an object but as a subject.

The Bible calls us not only servants but also friends of God.

Barth answers:—The objection which we have just heard is the exact antithesis of what I said this morning. The speaker would have done better not to introduce his objection with a word of acknowledgment and gratitude to follow it up with a "but." He ought to have said, You are wrong! For then he would have understood me. We should have squarely faced each other. But if a man feels obliged to add to his endorsement a small "but" and a tiny "it seems to me," he has understood nothing at all. My friends, let me tell you that in the many discussions which I have had in nigh unto twenty years, I have heard over and over, first a friendly assent and then a "but." A small back door was opened through which everything that was to be eliminated was invited in again. If we are to face each other squarely, you must not meet me with such a "Yes, but—"; you must answer with a complete and unequivocal No!

But let us meet the objection itself. My whole address was meant to be altogether different from what you believe to have understood. It is most certainly not my idea that

there are two Gods. I thought to have done
everything to make clear that we are dealing
with one God and Lord. God the Reconciler
is also God the Creator. But do you mean to
say that to believe in God the Creator means
to believe that man is not as badly off as he
really is? So that it is possible to say: God
and man? You spoke of Christ. Let me emphasize only one fact. Christ believed He
could not bring real and genuine help to man
except by dying for him. What does it mean?
What shall we infer concerning man? Concerning ourselves? In the face of this fact, in
the face of the cross and resurrection of Christ,
what shall we assert of man except that man,
as man and without Christ, is lost. And to be
lost does not mean to have gone astray a little,
it means to be wholly lost. "This thy brother
was dead and is become alive again." What is
done to us, God in action for us, is a divine
miracle. What He does He does for the man
whom He has created, yes; but it is done to him
by the miracle of divine mercy. And if it is
true that we are met in mercy, what occasion
is there of speaking of cooperation? I did not
say that man is not a subject also. But, according to the Holy Scriptures, matters have come

to such a pass that this subject can only be helped by the intercession of another. I believe we need to learn anew what the Holy Scriptures say and mean by substitution of Jesus Christ and satisfaction. "I live, yet not I, Christ liveth in me!" In His face, it is impossible even so much as to mention cooperation. Certainly, we are neither stones nor beasts. We are human beings, even very nice people. But Christ was not able to help us in any other way than by dying for us. There is no other help for us than this. I invite you, not to form your estimate of man arbitrarily but to be guided by what the Holy Scriptures say of Him. If you will do this for a while, we shall understand each other better. And you will not feel compelled to suggest the correction which your question offers. You will gain a better understanding—not of my theology, which is not necessary—but of the whole view of life which I am speaking; or you will—it is the other possibility—refuse it altogether. What is needed above all today is a clear and unequivocal stand: Yes or No! The Church will die if we continue in our mere opinions. We must have the courage again to confess— or the courage to contradict!

A gentleman from China presents with deep emotion an extended vote on the realization of the kingdom of God on earth in general and offers five questions in detail.

Barth answers:—I confess that I am deeply moved by what our friend from China has said. A spirit of impatience rang through his address, and I wish every one of us had something of his impatience in him. Every one of his five questions gives evidence that he is visibly moved by the misery of human life. And now he sees in the face of all this misery—the Church. Ought not the Church interfere much more energetically? Ought it not find, and give, an answer? And, wrathfully, he seems to sense in my address a denial. Let me assure you that your protest would be absolutely justified if you were correct in your assumption. But are we not after all dealing with his questions? Is it not true that if we see men suffer we rightfully look about for help? And is it not true that we are right in laying hold of the gospel and in making an appeal to the Church? There can be no doubt that these questions are to be answered only in the affirmative.

To what end is the Church? What do reconciliation and deliverance mean, if they do not mean reconciliation and deliverance of these unhappy people? What sense would the petition in the Lord's prayer have, "Thy kingdom come," if it did not mean: Thy kingdom come to us, into our dark and dreary world? Create thou a new heaven and a new earth! What would the hope of faith mean if it is not a real hope for a very real liberty? Dear friend, we are agreed if this passionate hope and prayer is in your mind which says, Come Lord Jesus, come!—a prayer in which everyone may join in the misery of life. And, I believe that whoever stands with uplifted hands in the face of the injustices in the world, will be a passionately agitated man and very active in life.

Let me tell you this: Once I was a religious socialist. I discarded it because I believed I saw that religious socialism failed to take as serious and profound a view of man's misery, and of the help for him, as do the Holy Scriptures. I do not wish to say that your contention is wrong. I would like to affirm it. But I invite you to be even more serious and profound than you are now. As we read the Bible, we read a bit of human history. We read a good deal of injustice and bloodshed in it. But have you never found it remarkable how little weight is attached to it? We are simply told, man is lost; he is dead in his sins. Few words for a long, long story; but they tell the whole story. It is a very serious view of man's misery. It is the misery of one who has departed from God, fights against Him, and is His enemy in whatever He does. But here you are shown also a help by which man is really and truly helped. It is a radical help, because God Himself intercedes for this man.

I do not ask you to eliminate your questions, but I urge you to become even more of a radical. If you will do this, your various questions will head up into one comprehensive question. Why do we still suffer oppression? Yes, why? Shall we be surprised at what is going on in the world if we have an ear for what the Holy Scriptures tell us of man? Shall we be surprised *if* we know Jesus Christ who died for us, and if we then take a look at ourselves? We can and we ought to be surprised. But if we are surprised, the question is really answered. It is not man's own will that will help him. His help comes from the Lord who made heaven and earth.

And as to your question. Is there a Church of God?—I *believe* in a holy catholic apostolic

Church. It is this Church that is the Church of God. The question may be inverted, however, and then *we* are asked, Are *you* a member of this Church? Where we take a really serious and realistic invoice of man's misery and of the help which has come to him, we shall be given to see something of this Church. But it is a gift of God, and we must receive it ever anew.

And as to your inquiry about the sacrament, it must be said that the sacrament signifies most assuredly a material participation in the life of God. But it is truly God's gift which we must approach with *empty* hands to let God fill them. And as to your final question, how the kingdom of God comes in the earth, whether by preaching or by social activity, I would answer: The kingdom of God comes through God Himself who makes all things new. And it is perhaps of lesser importance to debate whether we should preach or devote ourselves to social work than to comprehend and carry on this prayer in our hearts: *Thy* kingdom come! *Thy* will be done!

❋   ❋   ❋

A gentleman from India thinks man's answer to God's action ought to be more strongly emphasized. He is of the opinion that it is hardly possible to make a start in India with "It is written!" It is necessary to take cognizance of India's background and its peculiar needs.

Barth answers: It is both moving and interesting that the response of this circle to what I have tried to say this morning does not differ from the response of others. The other side is urged with a goodly measure of passionate emphasis. Let me ask our friend from India —and I am asking many others also: Whence this passion? Whence this zeal? Not only God but also *I*, the man, who is also in the picture and who gets better treatment in the Scriptures than from Barth! Do you ever find in the Bible a situation where a man has this passion? Did it ever occur to you that the Bible always speaks in the direction in which I attempted to speak this morning? Certainly, the Bible speaks of man. But the relation between God and man is always the relation of a superior to a subordinate. Insubordination is never in the picture.

You consider me too severe, too one-sided. Perhaps I am one-sided. But, please, do not hold me responsible for that. Tell me a single prophet, or apostle, or Reformer, who has done differently from what I am trying to do with my weak strength. What is the relation which exists between God and man according to the Bible? Certainly, two principals are involved. But the Bible has no room for a man who plays the role of an independent partner! The Bible speaks of man as a child of God, as of one who belongs to Christ and is already redeemed. According to the Bible, it is God who reached out for man. If the Christian witness meets other men he ought to think that Christ has died for them also. For this reason, and for this reason alone, does any man belong to God.

To be sure, there is another possibility. The Bible sees it only as the shadow of this light, however. It is not unaware of the man who hardens his heart and refuses to acknowledge the gospel. But this kind of a man appears only as an impossible man. The man on whom the Bible looks as a genuine man is God's child who speaks to God as to his Father. All dealings between God and man take place within a circle which God has closed. The very man who acknowledges God does not feel the need of asserting himself against God. He will only want to acknowledge: Thou, and Thou alone, art the God who can help me, hast helped me, and wilt help me again. You spoke of India. I never was in India and I do not know how one must speak to the people of India. But I do know a little of how one speaks to men in general, to men who are sinners and who need to be redeemed by the divine miracle. And so I can only say, Certainly, it is necessary to speak to men of this miracle in the language which they understand, whether German, or French, or Chinese, or Hindu. But what will you tell them except by grace of grace? Is it possible to address a man first as a heathen, or is it not rather indicated to address the man in India also as a man for whom Christ has already done everything? I can only call the heathen into the fellowship of Christ if I believe that he is already in Christ. It is not I that places him under grace. He is there because Christ has already placed him there. You understand that for this reason all my labors on behalf of man as such falls away. We can only work for this man as for one who is already in Christ. And if this is granted, you do not need to search for point of contact, a connection link, because the connection has long since been established. It is, however, the task of a Christian witness to call to mind this connection.

* * *

A Russian professor tells the story of the suffering and death of an archbishop during the Revolution which became to him a testimony. His aim is to prove that witnessing is more far-reaching than Barth will have it. It extends not only to words but also to deeds and suffering.

Barth answers: We must come to a close. But this discussion could continue indefinitely. To what has been said just now, I would only remark that the New Testament knows nothing of a Church which is purified and washed in the blood of martyrs. On the whole—and I cannot help it—the word testimony is never used for what martyrs do and suffer. The New Testament does not set off and magnify martyrs. This tendency belongs to a later age, about the time of Ignatius. The New Testament reports the death of only one martyr, Stephen. It is his *sermon,* however, which makes him a witness, and not his suffering. The Church is washed and purified by the blood

of Jesus Christ alone. This is what the Bible
says, whether we like it or not. Take issue with
this fact and consider what it signifies for the
concept of witness and testimony.

*   *   *

A series of questions are asked which run in
the direction of the objections previously
voiced: Barth's address confines the concept
of witness to too narrow a limit; it needs to be
supplemented and integrated in respect to life.

Barth answers: In looking at the situation
in which I am facing you, I feel like a man
who is making a vain attempt to swim against
a torrent. It is quite evident that this conference is against me. Were I to use a biblical
picture, I would compare my mood with that
of the prophet Jonah in Nineveh. Or to em-
ploy a parable from nature: A gust of wind
blows across a grainfield. For a moment the
ears bend low. But already they are rising
again. I shall not follow the prophet's example, however, under this beautiful tree which
God has planted. I shall try to reply without
anger, even if you persist in contradicting me.
It must be so.

For a beginning I do not care to enter into
a discussion of the several arguments. There

is one objection common to you all. Let me
enlarge a bit with a more general exposition.
My friends, by all means do not think that I
am merely propounding a theory which I have
put in my head. The words "abstract" and
"theoretical" escaped you. You may rest assured that I have a little experience of my
own. I am a modern man also, and I stand
in the midst of this age, too. I see its problems, as do others. You really do not need
to instruct me so violently that what we are
concerned about is life. No, I must live a life,
not merely in theory but in practice, and live
it in the midst of a very stormy present. And
I assure you, exactly in life, exactly because
I was called to live in a modern world, did I
reach the path of which you have heard me
speak.

Perhaps I may describe to you the beginning
of my ways in order to tell you later what I
think of your objections. For ten years I was
a pastor. I faced the task of preaching the
gospel. I met the problem with which every
one of you is well acquainted: secularism. I
saw a modern world. And in this modern
world I saw a Church also. But it was a Church
which patently is following rules other than

those which, in the Holy Scriptures, we believe to recognize as Christian rules. A few
years ago this problem of secularism stood in
the forefront of every discussion. In this Christian world, which has turned secular I saw
further, a Church, a Christianity, which, with
great sincerity, with fervent zeal, with great
inwardness, and with fervid devotion to deeds
of charity, was only too closely related to the
modern world which surrounded it. For this
modern church—in Switzerland, in Germany,
and most likely in all other lands also—did not
raise up a sanctuary in the world; for this
Church did no longer know what sacrament
means; for it did no longer know that, as God
and the world come face to face, *God* must
help the world; for the Church, in fact its best
representatives, stood for the doctrine: men
and the world must be helped by love, by what
Christians possess, by what they are, and by
what they have to say and carry into the world
of men from out of their gospel treasuries.

And they proceeded to fit their actions to
their ideas with evangelization and works of
charity, with social activity, and, in our own
day, with the remarkable fusion of Christianity
and nationalism. All along the line, it was a

Church which was no longer Church, and did not care to remain any longer the Church of God. It was, and meant to be, the Church of the pious man, the Church of the good man, the Church of the moral man, but, at any rate, the Church of *man*.

And now I maintain that this modern Church is a near relative of the Godless modern world. It is the reverse side of this world. What the world did when it tore itself loose from God, the Church, and modern Christianity did and still does. There came a time in my life when this fact shocked and terrified me. I, too, have traveled the road which you indicate to me. I have tried about everything in this field. But there came a day when fear struck my heart. For I found something else in the Bible, something altogether different from the world's godlessness, but no less different from the godlessness of the Church and Christianity. I shall not now enlarge on what I found.

As I listen to you, I am strongly reminded of a definite period in the history of the Christian Church. About two hundred years ago, Christianity and the Church felt called upon to make the great discovery with which you

oppose me: Not only doctrine but life also!
Not only the Word but charity and our good
deeds also! It was at the beginning of the
eighteenth century when Pietism rose up
against the orthodoxy of the sixteenth and
seventeenth centuries. There was much truth
in the protest and criticism which the new age
heaped upon its predecessor. From the Reformation, the Church had heard of God and of
Christ. And now, one hundred and fifty years
later, it became apparent that something was
wrong. There was preaching, yes, and good
preaching, too. But love was not active. And
men were struck with fear. They cast anxious
eyes about them as they recalled the Thirty
Years' War and as they thought of the dark
and barren seventeenth century. It was then
that the fatal error was committed. They did
not say to themselves: Let us gain a *better*
understanding! Let us give *better* heed! Let
God be even more *God,* and let Christ be even
more *the Christ!* Let us take our journey
from our baptism to the Lord's Supper in an
even more serious way. Instead of this, they
said among themselves: Let us improve matters *ourselves!* Let *us* cultivate the Christian
life! They turned aside from the living God

and began to cultivate in a very sincere, very worthy, and very pious manner what we see before us in full bloom: the pious man. But slowly and logically, reverence of the pious man changed to reverence of what? the moral man! And finally, when it was found that man is of so large an importance, it became less important to speak of God, of Christ, and of the Holy Spirit. In their place, men began to speak of human reason.

And now let me tell you something from our immediate present day. My dear friends from England and America, I am from Germany. There we have reached the end of the road at whose beginning you are standing. If you begin to take the pious *man* serious, if you do not care to be one-sided, you will reach the same end before which the official German Church stands today. For what we have experienced in Germany during these latter days —this remarkable apostasy of the Church to nationalism, and I am sure that every one of you is horrified and says in his heart: I thank thee God that I am not a German Christian! I assure you it will be the end of your road, too. It has its beginning with "Christian *life*" and ends in paganism. For, if you once admit,

"Not only God but I also," and if your heart is with the latter—and friends, that's where you have it!—there is no stopping it. Let me assure you that there are many sincere and very lovely people among the German Christians. But it did not save them from falling a prey to this error. Let me warn you now. If you make a start with "God *and* . . ." you are opening the doors to every demon. And the charge which I raise against you I lay before you in the words of Anselm: Tu non considerasti, quandi ponderis sit peccatum! You failed to consider the weight of sin! And this is the sin: that man takes himself so very seriously. You are not yet forced to think on these things. Perhaps it is still possible in your Churches to carry on discussions about them. The enemy has not yet made his appearance, at least, not as he has invaded Germany—as the man who has risen to claim his rights, recklessly and brutally. What will you do if a similar fate befall you? Will you face the enemy with the weapons you are now carrying in your hands? Let me assure you in advance that you will never stand before him. In Germany we have learned by experience that the one thing that offered a chance to face the real enemy and refuse his claim was the simple message: God is the only Helper! It was the simple Either-Or which was refused a while ago. Learn in time what may here be learned. You are still soldiers in the barracks. Real firing has not yet begun for you. Some day you may be called to the front line. Perhaps there you will remember our discussion. You may then gain a better understanding of what you do not seem to be able to grasp today. One-sidedness will be your only chance.

*   *   *

A student from Czechoslovakia introduces the question of Christian ethics and amplifies the subject to the effect that general directives do not exist; but there is a demand for concrete decisions which as such are continually put under the divine judgment and divine grace.

Barth answers: Before I reply to this final question, I would like to take up a point which Mr. Maury has asked me to touch upon again. Let me explain once more the relation between what I called the modern Church and secularism. With this point I may well link up what Professor Zander said in regard to martyrdom. Historically, the way was as follows: the New

Testament does not regard martyrdom as testimony, as was done by a later age. The eleventh chapter of Hebrews was cited. But I invite you not to forget that the first verse reads: "Faith is the assurance of things hoped for, a conviction of things not seen." If the witnessing activity of martyrs is interpreted in the light of this verse, I assent. But, it differs widely from what the second century emphasized in martyrdom. In the meaning of the New Testament, it is the martyr's faith in the things unseen and not his suffering that makes him a witness. There is no more serious misconception of the large gift which the Church received in their martyrs than to make their *suffering* their testimony. History marched on. Martyrs ceased to be after a few centuries. Their vacant place as bearers of testimony was taken by the *life* of the Church. What would it mean, anyway, if it were really true that the life of the Church serves as testimony for God? Are we really so optimistic about it? Will not our suffering, will not our most devoted Christian life rather speak *against* Christ than for Him?

If the Church does not bear witness by erecting again a sanctuary, I am afraid there will be little or no testimony forthcoming. The world is not waiting for the noble things which we can show her, live and suffer before her; the world is waiting for Jesus Christ! It was very interesting that in one of the talks reference was made to "God in nature." If this is to be only a beginning where will you draw the line? Why should not race, or blood, or soil be of equal service. And would we then not be in the very midst of paganism? I love nature: I look on it as one of God's gifts. But the Church does not exist in order to proclaim nature, but Jesus Christ. This is what I call the connecting link between secularism and the modern Church. It begins with God and ends without God. And *necessarily* so!

And now a reply to the last, and indeed very serious, question. I have nothing to urge against it. It is quite self-evident that every man lives daily, in the larger and smaller interests of life, in constant decisions; *i.e.,* you must make answer to the word of God for your life. There is your court and your judge. Every individual and the Church as a whole must there, at that point, give answer for his existence. This is what Christian living means.

But we do not exist as atoms, every man for

himself. The decisions which we are called upon to make are made not merely between the Holy Scriptures and our human reason. We live as parts of the Church. We have a definite Christian tradition. We have passed through some definite Christian instruction. We have a catechism and a dogma. Definite insights have been passed on to us by the Church, and we may not ignore them. We have "fathers in the faith." The fourth commandment enters here and demands attention. To be sure, the fathers cannot relieve us of the responsibility of making our own decision. And hence arises the even larger problem, verily, the existential decision which we must make. It will drive us to decisions in every sphere of life, yes, politics included.

But now let me add just one more thought. The Church will need to be on guard lest the spirit of the age influence her decision. It is her greatest danger. If the Church will submit to this, it is a sign that she did not arrive at her decision in the presence of the Word of God. Against this danger the Church is compelled to counter with a peremptory "Hands off!" In times when such a spirit pervades the age, the Church must cry "Stop!" In such

times, it may even be better to say too little
than to say too much. The Church possesses a
way of executing her decision by simply devot-
ing herself to expounding her text. For example, if the Church in Germany were content
today merely to expound the Sermon on the
Mount it would not address itself directly to
National Socialism. And yet, it would be executing a decision in the meaning of the New
Testament. The Church's road lies through
the world. The Holy Scriptures has indicated
to it only one message. This message it is
bound to deliver. And in its light, every man
may know the decision he is called upon to
make. Whoever will lend his ear to the New
Testament today will certainly not be irreso-
lute. He will be glad that there is a higher
court of appeal to which he may flee if it should
become manifest that his decision was an error
after all. For even the best of us are subject
to error. For this reason, however, it is necessary that a sanctuary be built in the midst of
our world. And this sanctuary must not be a
hybrid of Church and world, it must be truly
Church, a Church which will remind men of
the eternal kingdom of God.